CAMPING for BOYS

About the author

H.W. Gibson first published *Camping for Boys* in 1913, having spent much of his life dedicated to the camping movement.

Transcriber's notes

This book shows a world where character and morality are prized. The goal of camp is not just to get the boys out of the parents' hair, but to encourage good character and citizenship. Camp leaders are enticed by the contribution they can make to the boys' futures and are selected (or rejected) based on their own moral virtues.

There are many practical suggestions for safety and comfort aside from the absence of modern materials and conveniences, like nylon and gas stoves.

Medical advice given in the book is from 1913 and may be unhelpful, often contradicts current practice and involves unsafe or now illegal substances.

The Heart of the Camp

Have you smelled wood smoke at twilight?
Have you heard the birch log burning?
Are you quick to read the noises of the night?
You must follow with the others for the young men's feet are turning
To the camps of proved desire and known delight.

From Kipling's 'Feet of the Young Men.'

CAMPING for BOYS

H.W. GIBSON

TEMPUS

To the thousand and more boys who have been my camp-mates in camps Shand, Durrell and Becket

First published 1913
Copyright © in this edition, Tempus, 2007

Tempus Publishing Limited
The Mill, Brimscombe Port,
Stroud, Gloucestershire, GL5 2QG
www.tempus-publishing.com

The right of H.W. Gibson to be identified as the Author
of this work has been asserted in accordance with the
Copyrights, Designs and Patents Act 1988.

British Library Cataloguing in Publication Data.
A catalogue record for this book is available from the British Library.

ISBN 978 0 7524 4311 9

Typesetting and origination by Tempus Publishing Limited
Printed and bound in Great Britain

Contents

Foreword

The author has conducted boys' camps for twenty-three years, so that he is not without experience in the subject. To share with others this experience has been his aim in writing the book. The various chapters have been worked out from a practical viewpoint, the desire being to make a handbook of suggestions for those in charge of camps for boys and for boys who go camping, rather than a theoretical treatise upon the general subject.

Thanks are due to E.M. Robinson, Dr Elias G. Brown, Charles R. Scott, Irving G. MacColl, J.A. Van Dis, Taylor Statten, W.H. Wones, H.C. Beckman, W.H. Burger, H.M. Burr, A.B. Wegener, A.D. Murray, and H.M. Allen, for valuable suggestions and ideas incorporated in many chapters.

Grateful acknowledgment is made to the following publishers for permission to quote from the books mentioned in the Bibliography: Charles Scribner's Sons, Harper Brothers, Outing Publishing Company, Baker & Taylor Company, Lothrop, Lee & Shepard Company, Penn Publishing Company, Doubleday, Page & Company, Hinds, Noble & Eldredge, Ginn & Company, Sunday School Times Company, G.P. Putnam's Sons, Little, Brown & Company, Moffat, Yard & Company, Houghton, Mifflin Company, Sturgis & Walton, Funk & Wagnall's Company, The Manual Arts Press, Frederick Warne & Company, Review and Herald Publishing Company, Health-Education League, Pacific Press Publishing Company.

Every leader, before going to camp, should read some book upon boy life, in order, not only that he may refresh his memory regarding his own boyhood days, but that he may also the more intelligently fit himself for the responsibility of leadership. The following books, or similar ones, may be found in any well-equipped library.

If this book will help some man to be of greater service to boys, as well as to inspire boys to live the noble life which God's great out-of-doors teaches, the author will feel amply repaid for his labour.

Boston, Mass., April, 1911.

I

The Purpose of Camping

It is great fun to live in the glorious open air, fragrant with the smell of the woods and flowers; it is fun to swim and fish and hike it over the hills; it is fun to sit about the open fire and spin yarns, or watch in silence the glowing embers; but the greatest fun of all is to win the love and confidence of some boy who has been a trouble to himself and everybody else, and help him to become a man.

(H.M. Burr)

The summer time is a period of moral deterioration with most boys. Free from restraint of school and many times of home, boys wander during the vacation time into paths of wrongdoing largely because of a lack of directed play life and a natural outlet for the expenditure of their surplus energy. The vacation problem therefore becomes a serious one for both the boy and his parent. Camping offers a solution.

The Need

A boy in the process of growing needs the outdoors. He needs room and range. He needs the tonic of the hills, the woods and streams. He needs to walk under the great sky, and commune with the stars. He needs to place himself where nature can speak to him. He ought to get close to the soil. He ought to be toughened by sun and wind, rain and cold. Nothing can take the place, for the boy, of stout physique, robust health, good blood, firm muscles, sound nerves, for these are the conditions of character and efficiency. The early teens are the most important years for the boy physically ... Through the ages of thirteen and fifteen the more he can be in the open, free from social engagements and from continuous labor or study, the better. He should fish, swim, row and sail, roam the woods and the waters, get plenty of vigorous action, have interesting, healthful things to think about.

(Prof. C.W. Votaw)

The Purpose

This is the real purpose of camping, 'something to do, something to think about, something to enjoy in the woods, with a view always to character-building', this is the way Ernest Thompson-Seton, that master wood-craftsman, puts it. Character building! What a great objective! It challenges the best that is in a man or boy. Camping is an experience, not an institution. It is an experience which every live, full-blooded, growing boy longs for, and happy the day of his realisation. At the first sign of spring, back yards blossom forth with tents of endless variety. To sleep out, to cook food, to search for nature's fascinating secrets, to make things – all are but the expression of that instinct for freedom of living in the great out-of-doors which God created within him.

Too Much House

'Too much house,' says Jacob Riis; 'Civilization has been making of the world a hothouse. Man's instinct of self-preservation rebels; hence the appeal for the return to the simple life that is growing loud.' Boys need to get away from the schoolroom and books, and may I say the martyrdom of examinations, high marks, promotions and exhibitions! Medical examinations of school children reveal some startling facts. Why should boys suffer from nerves? Are we sacrificing bodily vigour for abnormal intellectual growth? Have we been fighting against instead of cooperating with nature?

The tide is turning, however, and the people are living more and more in the open. Apostles of outdoor life like Henry D. Thoreau, John Burroughs, William Hamilton Gibson, Howard Henderson, Ernest Thompson-Seton, Frank Beard, Horace Kephart, Edward Breck, Charles Stedman Hanks, Stewart Edward White, 'Nessmuck,' W.C. Gray, and a host of others, have, through their writings, arrested the thought of busy people long enough to have them see the error of their ways and are bringing them to repentance.

Camps for boys are springing up like mushrooms. Literally thousands of boys who have heretofore wasted the glorious summer time loafing on the city streets, or as disastrously at summer hotels or amusement places, are now living during the vacation time under nature's canopy of blue with only enough covering for protection from rain and wind, and absorbing through the pores of their body that vitality which only pure air, sunshine, long hours of sleep, wholesome food, and reasonable discipline can supply.

Character Building

In reading over scores of booklets and prospectuses of camps for boys, one is impressed with their unanimity of purpose – that of character building. These are a few quotations taken from a variety of camp booklets:

The object of the camp is healthful recreation without temptation.

A camp where boys live close to nature, give themselves up to play, acquire skill in sports, eat plenty of wholesome food, and sleep long hours … and are taught high ideals for their own lives.

To give boys a delightful summer outing under favorable conditions, and to give them every opportunity to become familiar with camp life in all its phases. We believe this contributes much to the upbuilding of a boy's character and enables him to get out of life much enjoyment that would not otherwise be possible.

A place where older boys, boys of the restless age, may live a happy, carefree, outdoor life, free from the artificialities and pernicious influences of the larger cities; [a place where] all the cravings of a real boy are satisfied; [a place] where constant association with agreeable companions and the influence of well-bred college men in a clean and healthy moral atmosphere make for noble manhood; a place where athletic sports harden the muscles, tan the skin, broaden the shoulders, brighten the eye, and send each lad back to his school work in the fall as brown as a berry and as hard as nails.

A camp of ideals, not a summer hotel nor a supplanter of the home. The principal reason for its existence is the providing of a safe place for parents to send their boys during the summer vacation, where, under the leadership of Christian men, they may be developed physically, mentally, socially, and morally.

Whether the camp is conducted under church, settlement, Young Men's Christian Association, or private auspices, the prime purpose of its existence should be that of character building.

Because of natural, physical, social, educational, moral, and religious conditions, the boy is taught those underlying principles which determine character. The harder things a boy does or endures, the stronger man he will become; the more unselfish and noble things he does, the better man he will become.

No Rough-house

The day of the extreme 'rough-house' camp has passed. Boys have discovered that real fun does not mean hurting or discomforting others, but consists in making others happy. The boy who gets the most out of camp is the boy who puts the most into camp.

Mottoes

Many camps build their program of camp activities around a motto such as:
'Each for All, and All for Each'
'Help the Other Fellow,'
'Do Your Best,'
'Nothing Without Labour,'
'A Gentleman Always,' and
'I Can and I Will.'

Scout Law

Endurance, self-control, self-reliance, and unselfishness are taught the 'Boy Scouts' through what is called the 'Scout Law.'

1 A Scout's honour is to be trusted;
2 Be loyal;
3 Do a good turn to somebody every day;
4 Be a friend to all;
5 Be courteous;
6 Be a friend to animals;
7 Be obedient;
8 Be cheerful;
9 Be thrifty.

All these are valuable, because they contribute to the making of character.

In the conduct of a boys' camp there must be a definite clear-cut purpose if satisfactory results are to be obtained. A go-as-you-please or do-as-you-please camp will soon become a place of harm and moral deterioration.

Results

Camping should give to the boy that self-reliance which is so essential in the making of a life, that faith in others which is the foundation of society, that spirit of altruism which will make him want to be of service in helping other fellows, that consciousness of God as evidenced in His handiwork which will give him a basis of morality, enduring and reasonable, and a spirit of reverence for things sacred and eternal. He ought to have a better appreciation of his home after a season away from what should be to him the sweetest place on earth.

Leadership

The success or failure of a boys' camp depends upon leadership rather than upon equipment. Boys are influenced by example rather than by precept. A boys' camp is largely built around a strong personality. Solve the problem of leadership, and you solve the greatest problem of camping.

The Director

No matter how large or how small the camp, there must be one who is in absolute control. He may be known as the director, superintendent, or leader. His word is final. He should be a man of executive ability and good common sense. He should have a keen appreciation of justice. A desire to be the friend and counsellor of every boy must always govern his action. He will always have the interest and welfare of every individual boy at heart, realising that parents have literally turned over to his care and keeping, for the time being, the bodies and souls of their boys. To be respected should be his aim. Too often the desire to be popular leads to failure.

Leaders

Aim to secure as assistant leaders or counsellors young men of unquestioned character and moral leadership, college men if possible, men of culture and refinement, who are good athletes, and who understand boy life.

> They should be strong and sympathetic, companionable men. Too much care cannot be exercised in choosing assistants. Beware of effeminate men, men who are morbid in sex matters. An alert leader can spot a 'crooked' man by his actions, his glances, and by his choice of favourites. Deal with a man of this type firmly, promptly, and quietly. Let him suddenly be 'called home by circumstances which he could not control.'

The leader must have the loyalty of his assistants. They should receive their rank from the leader, and this rank should be recognised by the entire camp. The highest ranking leader present at any time should have authority over the party.

In a boys' camp I prefer the term 'leader' to that of 'counsellor.' It is more natural for a boy to follow a leader than to listen to wise counsellors. 'Come on, fellows, let's – ' meets with hearty response. 'Boys, do this,' is an entirely different thing. Leaders should hold frequent councils regarding the life of the camp and share in determining its policy.

The most fruitful source of supply of leaders should be the colleges and preparatory schools. No vacation can be so profitably spent as that given over to the leadership of boy life. Here is a form of altruistic service which should appeal to purposeful college men. Older boys who have been campers make excellent leaders of younger boys. A leader should always receive some remuneration for his services, either carfare and board or a fixed sum of money definitely agreed upon beforehand. The pay should never be so large that he will look upon his position as a 'job.' Never cover service with the blinding attractiveness of money. The chief purpose of pay should be to help deepen the sense of responsibility, and prevent laxness and indifference, as well as to gain the services of those who must earn something.

Do not take a man as leader simply because he has certificates of recommendation. Know him personally. Find out what he is capable of doing. The following blank I use in securing information:

Leader's Information Blank,
Name
Address
College or school
Class of
Do you sing? What part (tenor or bass)?
Do you swim?
Do you play cricket? What position?
Do you play an instrument? What?
Will you bring it (unless piano) and music to camp?
Have you won any athletic or aquatic events? What?
Will you bring your school or college pennant with you?
Have you ever taken part in minstrel show, dramatics, or any kind of entertainment; if so, what?
What is your hobby? (If tennis, cricket, swimming, nature study, hiking, photography, athletics, etc., whatever it is, kindly tell about it in order to help in planning the camp activities.)

Leaders should not be chosen in order to secure a cricket team, or an athletic team. Select men of diverse gifts. One should know something about nature study, another about manual training, another a good story-teller, another a good athlete or cricket player, another a good swimmer, another a musician, etc.

Always remember, however, that the chief qualification should be moral worth.

Before camp opens it is a wise plan to send each leader a letter explaining in detail the purpose and program of the camp. A letter like the following is sent to the leaders of camps:

Suggestions to camp leaders. Read and re-read.

The success of a boys' camp depends upon the hearty cooperation of each leader with the superintendent. The boys will imitate you. A smile is always better than a frown. 'Kicking' in the presence of boys breeds discontent. Loyalty to the camp and its management is absolutely necessary if there is to be harmony in the camp life.

Personal

Your personal life will either be a blessing or a hindrance to the boys in your tent. Study each boy in your tent. Win his confidence. Determine to do your best in being a genuine friend of each boy. Remember in prayer daily each boy and your fellow leaders. Emphasise the camp motto, 'Each for all, and all for each.' Study the 'tests' on pages 8 and 9 of the booklets, and be helpful to the boys in your tent who are ambitious to improve and win the honour emblems.

Tents

Neatness and cleanliness must be the watchword of each tent. Sweets draw ants. Decayed material breeds disease. Insist upon the observance of sanitary rules.

It is unwise to have all the boys from one town or city in one tent. The tendency is to form clans, which destroy camp spirit. Get the fellows together the first thing and choose a tent name and tent yells.

Appoint a boy who will be responsible for the boys and the tent when you are not present.

Too much attention cannot be given to the matter of ventilation. When it rains, use a forked stick to hold the flaps open in the form of a diamond. In clear weather, tie one flap back at each end (flap toward the feet), allowing a free draft of air at all times. On rainy days encourage the boys to spend their time in the pavilion. Whenever possible, insist upon tent and blankets being thoroughly aired each morning.

Three inspectors will be appointed for each day; fifteen minutes' notice will be given and boys will not be allowed in or around their tents during the period of inspection. Leaders may suggest but not participate in arranging the tent.

The Honour Banner is to be given to the tent showing the best condition and held as long as marks are highest.

Swimming

The leader of swimming must give the signal before boys go into the water. Boys who cannot swim should be encouraged to learn. The morning dip must be a dip and not a swim.

Boats

No boats are to be taken unless an order has been issued by the tent leader (or by the superintendent). The man at the wharf always has power to veto orders at his discretion.

Order of Day

It is the leader's part to see that the order of the day is carried out and on time, including the setting up of drill. (See Camp Booklet.) 'Follow the leader' is an old game which is still influencing boys.

Work

Three tents and their leaders are responsible for the work at camp, and will be expected to report to the assistant superintendent after breakfast for assignment of work. These tents are changed each day, so that the boys and leaders come on duty only one day in seven.

Each tent is under its respective leader in doing the following work:

Tent 1 Sanitary work, such as policing the campus, emptying garbage cans, sweeping the pavilion, disinfecting, etc.

Tent 2 Preparing vegetables for the cook, drying dishes, pots, pans, cleaning up the kitchen, piazza, etc.

Tent 3 Cleaning the boats, supplying wood for the kitchen, putting ice in the refrigerator, etc.

The next day tents 4, 5 and 6 will come on duty, and so on until each tent has been on duty during the week.

Leaders for the day will call the squad together after breakfast and explain the day's plans. Encourage the boys to do this work cheerfully. Lead, do not drive the boys when working. Not more than three hours should be consumed in camp work.

Sports and Pastimes

Bring rule books on athletics. Study up group games. Bring any old clothes for costumes; tambourines and bones for minstrel show, grease paint, and burnt cork – in fact, anything that you think will add to the fun of the camp. Good stories and jokes are always in demand. Bring something interesting to read to your boys on rainy days. Think out some stunt to do at the social gatherings. If you play an instrument, be sure to bring it along with you.

Bank

Encourage the boys to turn their money and railroad tickets over to the camp banker instead of depositing them with you.

Camp Council

Meetings of the leaders will be held at the call of the superintendent. Matters talked over at the council meeting should not be talked over with the boys. All matters of discipline or anything that deals with the welfare of the camp should be brought up at this meeting. Printed report blanks will be given to each leader to be filled out and handed to the assistant superintendent each Thursday morning. Do not show these reports to the boys.

Bible Study

Each leader will be expected to read to the boys in his tent a chapter from the Bible and have prayers before 'taps' each night, also to take his turn in leading the morning devotions at breakfast table. Groups of boys will meet for occasional Bible study at sunset under various leaders. Each session will continue twenty minutes – no longer. Sunday morning service will be somewhat formal in character, with an address. The sunset vesper service will be informal.

Praying that the camp may prove a place where leaders and boys may grow in the best things of life and anticipating an outing of pleasure and profit to you, I am
Your friend,
(signature)

Opportunities

In securing men for leadership, impress upon them the many opportunities for the investment of their lives in the kind of work that builds character. In reading over a small folder, written by George H. Hogeman, I was so impressed with his excellent presentation of this theme of opportunities of leadership that the following is quoted in preference to anything I could write upon the subject:

The opportunity of the boys' camp leader is, first, to engage in the service that counts most largely in securing the future welfare of those who will soon be called upon to carry on the work that we are now engaged in. Most people are so busy with their own present enjoyment and future success that they pay little heed to the future of others. They may give some thought to the present need of those around them because it more or less directly affects themselves, but the work of character building in boys' camps is one that shows its best results in the years to come rather than in the immediate present.

In the second place, the opportunity comes to the camp leader to know boys as few other people know them, sometimes even better than their own parents know them. When you live, eat, sleep with a boy in the open, free life of camp for a month or so, you come in contact with him at vastly more points than you do in the more restrained home life, and you see sides of his nature that are seldom seen at other times.

Finally, the opportunity is given to the man who spends his vacation in camp to make the time really count for something in his own life and in the lives of others. To how many does vacation really mean a relaxation, a letting down of effort along one line, without the substitution of anything definite in its place! But he must be a dull soul, indeed, who can come to the right kind of boys' camp and not go away with his muscles harder, his eye brighter, his digestion better, and his spirit more awake to the things that pertain to the Kingdom of God.

Then again the camp leader must have the ability to forget himself in others. Nowhere can the real play spirit be entered into more completely than in camp life. A watchman is the last thing he must be. That spirit of unselfishness which forgets its own personal pleasure in doing the most for the general good, is the ideal camp spirit. As Lowell puts it in the Vision of Sir Launfal, it is:

'Not what we give, but what we share,
For the gift without the giver is bare.'

The results of all these points which I have mentioned are some very positive things. One is the very best kind of a vacation that it is possible to have. How frequently we hear in response to the question about enjoying a vacation, 'Oh, yes, I had a good enough time, but I'll never go back there again.' To my mind that indicates either that the person does not know what a really good time is, or that his surroundings made a good time impossible.

Another result of camp is the real friendships that last long after camping days are over. Of these I need not speak. You and I know of many such and what they mean in the development of Christian character in the lives of our men and boys. And, after all, there is the greatest result of all, the sense of confidence in the ultimate outcome that comes with having a share in the work of bringing others to the measure of the stature of the fullness of Christ.

The ideal life for a boy is not in the city. He should know of animals, rivers, plants, and that great out-of-door life that lays for him the foundation of his later years.

(G. Stanley)

Location and Sanitation

Dirt

Clean camps are most easily kept by not allowing them to become dirty.

> Cleanliness is next to Godliness. Godliness means a right relation to things spiritual, cleanliness a right relation to things material. An old definition says that 'Dirt is merely misplaced matter.' Of all the vehicles of disease, the most important perhaps is dirt. The word dirt in its strict sense comes from the Anglo-Saxon 'drit,' or excrement. 'Dirt,' then, is not earth or clean sand – not clean dirt, but dirty dirt, that is, matter soiled by some of the excreta of the human or animal body. Cleanliness must be insisted upon in a boys' Camp – not the cleanliness that makes a boy squeamish about working with his hands upon some necessary job, but cleanliness that makes him afraid of sharing his tooth brush or table utensils or his clothes.
>
> Cleanliness is not the shunning of good, clean dirt, but a recognition of the fact that to pass anything from one mouth to another is a possible source of death and destruction. [1]

'Death to dirt' should be the watchword of the camp. The camp should be a model of cleanliness. Every boy should be taught the value of good sanitation and encouraged to cooperate in making proper sanitation effective.

Avoid Swamps

The location chosen for a camp should be away from swamps. Avoid swampy and low places as you would a plague. Damp places where there are mosquitoes, should be well drained, and open to an abundance of sunshine. Mosquitoes breed only in water, but a very little water is sufficient if it is dirty and stagnant. Two inches of water standing in an old tin can will breed an innumerable horde. These 'diminutive musicians' are not only a nuisance, but dangerous, as malaria and typhoid spreaders by their poisonous stings.

The Site

In selecting a camp site bear in mind these things:

1 A sandy sub-soil, with good drainage. Avoid very sandy soil; sand provides but little hold for tent pegs, and there is grave risk of damage should there come a gale.
2 An open campus surrounded by hills or sheltering trees, and facing the water.
3 Plenty of good drinking water and water for swimming.
4 Base from which supplies and provisions are to be drawn should be within convenient distance, not more than four miles away.
5 Camp should be away from civilisation, far enough to be free from visitors and the temptation to 'go to town' on the part of the boys. Nothing demoralises a boys' camp so quickly as proximity to a summer resort.

Arrangement

Before opening the camp much thought and care should be given to its sanitary arrangement. First of all, the driest section of the camp ground should be selected for the erection of the sleeping tents. Locate them where they will have the full benefit of the sunshine. Tents erected under trees are liable to mildew, for the want of sunshine, and the contents of the tent will soon get musty. Next in importance to the location of 'quarters' is the location of the kitchen. This should be near the dining tent, so that the serving of food may be quick, and yet far enough away to insure that disagreeable odours will not destroy the pleasure of eating. If it is very near the sleeping tents the campers will be awakened too early by the chopping of wood and the necessary noises made in preparation of the morning meal. It should be near water. This is very essential for cooking and cleaning. In some of the large camps water is carried to the kitchen in pipes from near-by springs or pumped from wells of pure water. The dining quarters naturally should be located near the kitchen so that food may be served warm. Provision should be made for the protection of the boys from cold, wind, rain, and dampness while eating. The toilet should be located rather far away from the camp, and not in the direction from which the prevailing wind comes toward the camp. Make sure that it is on the line of opposite drainage from the water used by the camp. The details of laying out a camp, erection of tents, etc., are given in another chapter.

Latrines

Particular precaution should be exercised in location and care of the toilets or latrines, even in a one-night camp. Neglect of this will mean disease.

When on a one-night camp, dig a small pit which can be filled in again after use. If the camp is to be continued for a week or longer, dig a pit or trench about two or three feet deep and about eighteen inches wide, plant posts on each side of the trench, and eighteen inches above the ground level. Nail shaped seating on these posts. The number of seats will be determined by the size of the camping party. It is desirable to erect a six-foot canvas screen with an opening around the toilet. Dry earth should be sprinkled freely in the trench each time it is used. Also each morning sprinkle plenty of chloride of lime or some good, reliable disinfectant in the trench. Do not permit the throwing of paper about the toilet. Have a box in which paper is to be kept. Flies should be excluded by boxing up the sides of the seats and fastening a hinged lid upon the seats (see illustration). It is an advantage to admit the direct sunlight about the middle of the day because of its bactericidal action on disease germs. In a permanent camp regular wooden closets should be built, with covered roof for protection from rain and wind. The back of the closet should be arranged either by a hinged door or some other method so that the contents may be removed as often as once a week. A wooden box on rollers placed beneath the seats will facilitate removal. The seats should be scrubbed with hot water, sulpho-naphthol, or soap, daily. 'Springfield Oval' type of toilet paper prevents unnecessary waste. In one camp the water from a near-by brook is dammed and thus by gravity made to flow by a system of modern plumbing through the urinals and flush closets. This is ideal. Insist upon cleanliness. The cutting of initials and names upon the seats and woodwork should be considered a disgrace as well as a misdemeanour.

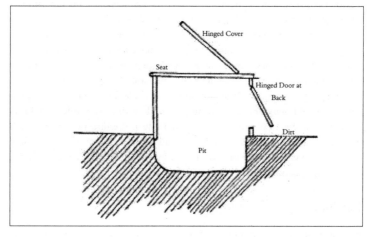

Pit toilet

Taboo the taking of books and papers to the toilet to read. It should be an imperative rule that no other place be used. A little carelessness will cause disagreeable as well as dangerous results. By way of reiteration: First, rigid prohibition of the pollution of the surface of the ground by the strictest rules, diligently enforced. Second, the provision of toilets or latrines of adequate size with proper precaution to prevent the dispersal of excreta by wind, flies, or other agencies. The latrines should be located a distance from camp but not so far as to offer temptation to pollution of the ground. Third, boys should be educated when on hikes or tramps in the old Mosaic Rule laid down in Deuteronomy 23: 12-14.[2]

Garbage

Garbage, consisting chiefly of trimmings of meat and vegetables and the waste from the table, if stored in open buckets soon becomes offensive and is an ideal breeding place in warm weather for flies 'that drink of cesspools, dine at privy vaults, eat sputum and are likely to be the most familiar guests at the dinner table, sampling every article of food upon which they walk, leaving in their tracks disease-producing germs which have adhered to their sticky feet where they have previously dined.' Declare war upon the 'fly who won't wipe his feet' by keeping the garbage in a covered galvanised-iron pail and dispose of it before decomposition takes place. Wash and dry the pail after emptying. If the camp is located near a farm, give the garbage to the farmer. It is the natural food of swine or poultry. Where this is not possible, the garbage should be buried every day in the earth and covered with three or four inches of dirt. Another and better plan, especially in a large camp, is the burning of the garbage and human excreta in an incinerator, such as the McCall. This is the method of the United States Army.

Exercise caution in throwing aside tin cans. The vegetable matter remaining in the cans soon decays and attracts flies. Have a place where these cans may be buried or burned with other refuse each day. Keep the ground surrounding the kitchen free from all kinds of garbage or refuse.

Do not throw dirty dish water promiscuously upon the ground. Dig a trench and put the water in this trench. Sprinkle chloride of lime or a disinfectant upon it each day. In a permanent camp a waste water well should be dug and lined with stone. The drain pipe should be laid from the kitchen to the well. This water soon disappears in the soil and does not become a nuisance. Make sure that the well is not in line with the water supply of the camp. A little potash or some washing soda dissolved in the sink will help to keep the drain clean.

Place barrels in different parts of the camp for refuse and scraps. A coat of whitewash or white paint will make them conspicuous. In one camp the following suggestive bit of verse was painted on the waste barrels:

Ravenous Barrel

I am all mouth and vacuum
I never get enough,
So cram me full of fruit peels,
Old papers, trash and stuff.

Epicurean Barrel

O, how sorry I feel for a boy
Who litters clean places with trash,
Who throws away papers and fruit peels
Which form my favourite hash.

Waste Barrels

These barrels should be set upon two strips of wood placed parallel. This permits the air to pass beneath the barrel and keeps its bottom from decaying by contact with the ground. The barrels should be emptied daily and the trash burned.

A dirty, carelessly kept, untidy camp will make discipline and order very difficult to attain and the influence will soon be noticed in the careless personal habits of the boys. There is an educational and moral value in cleanliness which is second only to that of good health.

Water Supply

Dr. Charles E.A. Winslow, the noted biologist, is authority for the following statement; ('Camp Conference', p.61):

The source of danger in water is always human or animal pollution. Occasionally we find water which is bad to drink on account of minerals dissolved on its way through the ground or on account of passage through lead pipes, but the danger is never from ordinary decomposing vegetable matter. If you have to choose between a bright, clear stream which may be polluted at some point above, and a pond full of dead leaves and peaty matter, but which you can inspect all around and find free from contamination, choose the pond. Even in the woods it is not easy to find surface waters that are surely protected, and streams particularly are dangerous sources of water supply. We have now got rid of the idea that running water purifies itself. It is standing water which purifies itself, if anything, for in stagnation there is much more chance for the disease germs to die out. Better than either a pond or stream, unless you can carry out a rather careful exploration of their surroundings, is ground water from a well or spring; though that again is not necessarily safe. If the well is in good sandy soil with no cracks or fissures, even water that has been polluted may be well purified and made safe to drink. In a clayey or rocky region, on the other hand, contaminating material may travel for considerable distance under ground. Even if your well is protected below, a very important point to look after is the pollution from the surface. I believe more cases of typhoid fever from wells are due to surface pollution than to the character of the water itself. This is a danger which can, of course, be done away with by protection of the well from surface drainage, by seeing that the surface wash is not allowed to drain toward it and that it is protected by a tight covering from the entrance of its own waste water. If good water cannot be secured in any of these ways, the water must be purified. It has been said that what we desire in water supply is innocence and not repentance; but if you cannot get pristine innocence, you can, at least, secure works meet for repentance and make the water safe, by filtering through either a Pasteur or a Berkefeld filter – either of those filters will take out bacteria, while no other filters that I know of will or by various chemical disinfectants, not any of them very satisfactory – or, best of all, by boiling, which will surely destroy all disease germs.

Indians had a way of purifying water from a pond or swamp by digging a hole about one foot across and down about six inches below the water level, a few feet from the pond. After it had filled with water, they bailed it out quickly, repeating the bailing process about three times. After the third bailing the hole would fill with filtered water. Try it.

Drinking Cups

Insist upon the boys bringing to camp a supply of inexpensive paper cups or collapsible pocket drinking cups. Filthy and dangerous diseases are not infrequently transmitted by the use of a common drinking cup.

Paper Drinking Cup

Take a piece of clean paper about 6 inches square and fold it on the dotted lines, as shown in Figure 1 overleaf, so as to make a triangle. Do not use paper having anything printed on it, as there is danger of poison from the ink. The other folds are made in the dotted lines, as shown in Figure 2. Each pointed end of the triangle is turned over on one side, as shown in Figure 3, then the sheets of the remaining points are separated and each one folded down on its respective side. This practical idea is furnished by R.H. Lufkin in *Popular Mechanics* for February 1911.

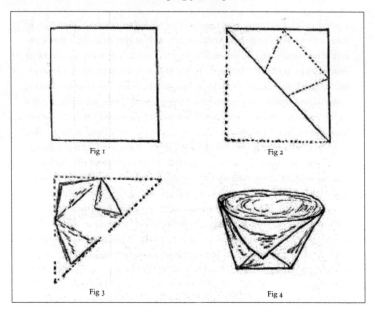

Fig 1   Fig 2

Fig 3   Fig 4

A paper drinking cup

Board of Health

Boys should be encouraged to cooperate in keeping the camp clean. A Board of Health may be organised, to be composed of an equal number of boys and camp leaders with the camp physician, or director of the camp as chairman.

The duties of the board will be to inspect daily the toilets, sinks, and drains, the water supply, the garbage disposal and waste barrels; condemn everything that is unsanitary, and correct all sanitary disorders. The board will also arrange for a series of talks upon 'Sanitation and Health', such as:

Sunshine and Health
Johnnie and the Microbes
Dirt and Cleanliness
Fresh Air
Flies and Filth
Health – Its Value and Its Cost.

Have the boys write essays upon these subjects and give credits or points for original interpretation, accuracy of report of talk given, and observance and correction of sanitary disorders.

Maxims

Clean up as you go. Sunshine and dryness are great microbe killers. It is better to keep clean, than to get clean. Dirt, dampness and disease can often be avoided by decency, dryness and determination. Uncleanness is at the root of many of the evils which cause suffering and ill health. Fire is the best disinfectant. Typhoid fever and cholera are carried by dirty habits, by dirty water and dirty milk.

Bibliography

Camp Sanitation – Review and Herald Pub. Assn., Washington, D.C. A twelve-page folder of useful hints on what to do and what not to do.

Wastes and Their Disposal – Henry J. Barnes, M.D. Health-Education League, Boston, Mass. An authoritative booklet written by the Professor of Hygiene, Tufts Medical School. This League publishes a number of very valuable and comprehensive booklets on health subjects.

Good Health – Francis Gulick Jewett. Ginn and Co. Gives detail instruction in matters of health and hygiene. Prepared especially for younger people.

Health – B. Franklin Richards. Pacific Press Pub. Co. Written in language easily understood and filled with sensible suggestions.

4

Camp Equipment

The greatest help after all is to take the children back to the garden that the Lord God planted. A boy must learn to sleep under the open sky and to tramp ten miles through the rain if he wants to be strong.

(Edward Everett Hale)

Selecting a camp site and general directions for the laying out of the camp grounds is treated very fully in the chapter on Camp Sanitation, so that this chapter will be devoted to methods that to the experienced camper may seem trite, but which the novice will appreciate.

Advance Party

If the camp is a large one it is usually customary to send an advance party several days ahead to erect the tents and get the camp in readiness for the larger party. The successful management of a camp depends very much upon placing the tents in such a position as to give plenty of room and yet be compact. When tents are scattered the difficulty of control is increased. The above diagram is a suggestion for the laying out of a camp which provides for room and control.

Plan of Grounds

The following hints will help the advance party to lay out the camp in a systematic and scientific manner. To find the right angle of the camp square, drive a peg at A, another 3 feet distant at B; attach a 5-foot cord from the peg at B, and a 4 foot cord from the peg at A. The point at which the two cords meet at C, where another peg may be driven in, will be the line at right angles to B-A.

Measuring Device

The illustrations overleaf show a device by which a camp, cricket grounds, running track, tennis court or any distance may be quickly and accurately measured.

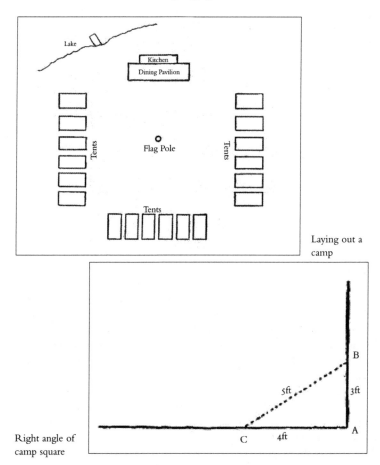

Laying out a camp

Right angle of camp square

The first thing to do is to get an inch board and cut a round disc 'a' about 12 inches in diameter. Cut two of them and tack them together. The diagram 'b' is easier to cut out and will serve the purpose just as well. When the two are temporarily tacked together, bore a hole through the centre for the axle. The eight spokes should be of light material and not too pointed or they will sink in the ground and prevent accuracy. The spokes are tacked on one disc as shown in 'c' and then the other disc is nailed on the outside.

Paint the end of one spoke red, so that you can count it every time it comes around. By having the points that touch the ground exactly 9 inches apart, one revolution of the wheel will measure six feet. For an axle use a small piece of broom handle, and for a handle use a long light pole. By varying the length of the spokes you can make the wheel measure any desired distance.

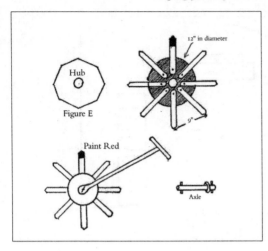

A measuring device

Wall Tent

The line of the camp having been laid out, the next thing is the erection of the tents. The best way of setting up a wall tent (either the 12 x 14 or 14 x 16 size), the type used in most of the boys' camps, is the method used by the army and described in Kephart's *Book of Camping and Woodcraft*. Four boys or men proceed as follows: Nos. 1 and 2 procure canvas, and Nos. 3 and 4 the poles.

Nos. 3 and 4 lay the ridge pole on the ground, in the direction that the tent is to stand; then lay the uprights at each end of ridge-pole and at right angles to it, on the side opposite that from which the wind blows. Then drop the tent pins and hammers at their respective ends of the tent; then drive a pin at each end of the ridge to mark front and rear. Meanwhile Nos. 1 and 2 unroll the tent and spread it out over the ridge-pole and on both sides of it.

Nos. 1 and 3 now go to the rear, and Nos. 2 and 4 to the front, and slip the pins of the uprights through the ridge-pole and tent. If a fly is used, it is placed in position over the tent, and the loops of the long guys over the front and rear pole pins. No. 4 secures centre (door) loops over centre pin in front, and No. 1 in rear. Each goes to his corner, No. 1 right rear, No. 2 right front, No. 3 left rear, No. 4 left front.

All draw bottom of tent taut and square, the front and rear at right angles to the ridge, and fasten it with pins through the corner loops, then stepping outward two paces from the corner, and a pace to the front (Nos. 2 and 4) or rear (Nos. 1 and 3) each securely sets a long pin, over which is passed the extended corner guy rope. Care must be taken that the tent is properly squared and pinned to the ground at the door and four corners before raising it.

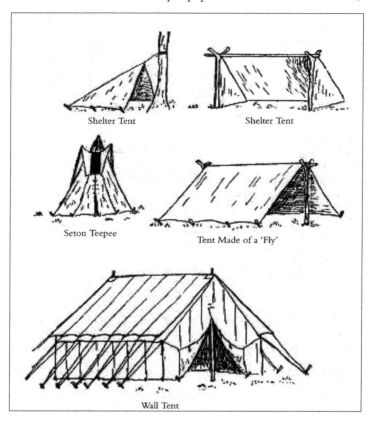

Shelter Tent

Shelter Tent

Seton Teepee

Tent Made of a 'Fly'

Wall Tent

Nos. 1 and 3 now go to the rear, and Nos. 2 and 4 to the front pole, and raise the tent to a convenient height from the ground, when Nos. 2 and 3 enter and seize their respective poles, and all together raise the tent until the upright poles are vertical. While Nos. 2 and 3 support the poles, Nos. 1 and 4 tighten the corner guys, beginning on the windward side. The tent being thus temporarily secured, all set the guy pins and fasten the guy ropes, Nos. 1 and 2 to the right, Nos. 3 and 4 left, and then set the wall pins.

To prevent the upright poles from sinking in the ground under the pressure of the canvas, place a flat stone or piece of wood under the pole.

Guying the Tent

One of the troubles with tents is their remarkable proclivity for tightening and slackening with the varying conditions of the weather. This means a constant loosening or tightening of the guy ropes, and the longer the guy ropes the more they will shrink or stretch according as they are wet or dry. This may be overcome to some extent by using very heavy corner posts securely driven into the ground and spiking a pole across them, and very short guy ropes fastening to this pole. A shower, or even ordinary dew, will cause the canvas to shrink, therefore be sure to slacken the guys, or you may have a torn tent or broken ridge pole.

Trenching

Dig a trench around the tent and do it before you have to. If you have ever gotten out in the middle of the night when the rain was coming down in torrents, to dig a ditch or trench, you will appreciate this bit of advice.

Warn the boys not to touch the roof of the tent on the inside when it is raining, for it will surely leak wherever it is touched.

There is a right and a wrong way of driving stakes into the ground. Study illustrations.

Peg Wisdom

In taking down the tent, don't pound loose the tent pins or pegs, but with a looped rope and a pull in the direction from which they are driven they can easily be removed.

Conveniences

After pitching your tent, put everything in order. Run a stout line, either of rope or rustless wire, between the two upright poles, about a foot below the ridge pole. A very convenient thing to throw clothes over. In some camps they have a shelf suspended from the ridge pole, divided into compartments, one for each boy in the tent. Nails driven in the upright poles afford convenient pegs to hang things on. Be sure the nails are removed before taking down the tent or a rip in the canvas will be the result.

A bundle of elder leaves in a tent will keep away flies. If ants show a desire to creep into your tent, dust cayenne pepper into their holes and they will no longer trouble you.

When there is no wooden floor in the tent, strew small hemlock twigs. They make a fine carpet and the odour is both pleasant and healthful.

In addition to the different styles of tents shown in the illustrations on page 29, the following description of how to make a ten-foot teepee is given by Charles R. Scott in his Vacation Diary:

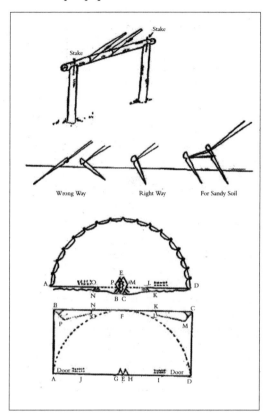

The ten-foot teepee

Making a Teepee

Sew canvas together making oblong ABCD 20 by 10 feet; with E as centre and EA as a radius, draw half-circle AFD. From remaining canvas cut smoke flaps LKCM and ONBP. Sew piece of canvas at C and B making pocket for ends of smoke poles. Sew ML to HI and PO to GJ on one large piece of canvas. Sew lash to E to tie teepee to pole. Sew 6 or 7-foot lash to K and N to set smoke flaps with. Make holes in pairs from L to D and O to A for lacing pins. Ten poles 12 feet long are needed. Make tripod of nine of these and tie teepee at E to pole two feet from top and place over tripod.

In Recreation April 1911, in an article on 'Tent Making Made Easy,' H.J. Holden tells how to make ten different tents with but one piece of canvas.

Tent Wisdom

The best type of tent to use in a permanent camp is a wall tent, either 12 x 14 or 14 x 16, which will accommodate from four to six fellows. An eight ounce, mildew-proofed duck, with a ten or twelve ounce duck fly will give excellent wear. Have a door at each end of the tent and the door ties made of cotton cord instead of tape. Double pieces of canvas should be sewed in all the corners and places where there is unusual strain. Manilla rope is best for guys, and metal slides are preferable to wood. If the tents are made to order, have a cotton cord about two feet long sewed in each seam just under the eaves, so that one end shall hang down inside the tent and the other outside. The walls of the tent can then be rolled up and tied so that the tent will be thoroughly aired. Make sure that the end of the ridge pole and of the upright poles have iron bands to prevent splitting of the poles.

Bed on Ground

For a short-term camp, pine boughs make the best kind of a bed (see chapter on Tramps and Hikes for description of bed). Sometimes a rubber blanket is spread upon the ground and the boys roll themselves up in their blankets. An old camper gives the following suggestion to those who desire to sleep in this fashion: 'The bed should be made in the afternoon while the sun is shining. To make the bed, clear the ground of twigs and stones. The space should be about 6 x 3 feet.'

A 'Hip Hole'

A shovelful of dirt is removed, making a shallow, transverse trench, about midway of the bed. This trench is the 'hip hole' and the making of it properly is what renders the bed comfortable. In making the bed the following order should be observed:

1 spread the rubber blanket;
2 the blanket spread so that one-half only covers the prepared couch;
3 then spread the woollen blankets so that the 'hip hole' is in the right place;
4 add the pillow;
5 fold the blankets over you and pin them with big safety pins across the bottom and along the side.

To Keep Warm

Stewart Edward White in *Camp and Trail* tells how to keep warm when sleep-ing on the ground:

> Lie flat on your back. Spread the blanket over you. Now raise your legs rigid from the hip, the blanket, of course, draping over them. In two swift motions tuck first one edge under your legs from right to left, then the second edge under from left to right, and over the first edge. Lower your legs, wrap up your shoulders and go to sleep. If you roll over, one edge will unwind but the other will tighten.

A bed tick[1] 6-1/2 feet long and 2-1/2 feet wide, to be filled with grass, leaves, straw or any available stuff makes a comfortable bed.

To Make a Bed

A comfortable bed is made by driving four posts in the ground and nailing a framework of saplings on these posts. Rope is then interwoven from side to side in somewhat the fashion of the old-time cord bed. Pine boughs are then placed 'shingle' fashion in the cording, making a very comfortable bed.

Double-Deck Bunks

Many of the long-term camps, however, have cots or bunks with canvas bot-toms. This is the best way to sleep for boys who are going to be in camp the entire summer. The following type of double-deck bunk is in use at camps. The illustrations give a clear idea of its construction. Use wood as free from knots as possible. Spruce seems to be the best kind as it is both light in weight and very durable. The top section upon which the canvas beds are tacked is bolted to the uprights which makes a bunk easily taken apart. Three of these uprights, one at each end and one in the middle, will make a bed section accommodating four boys, two on the 'first floor' and two on the 'second floor.' In this manner eight boys may be comfortably housed in a 12 x 14 or 14 x 16 foot tent, with room for baggage in the centre.

Blankets

Always remember that to keep warm while sleeping in a cot or bunk, you must have as much thickness of blanket under you as above you. Usually boys will pile blankets on top of them and have only one blanket under them and then wonder why they are cold.

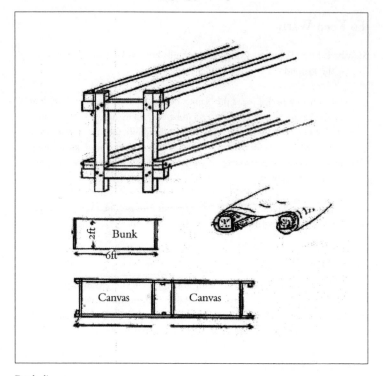

Bunk diagram

Pillows

A pillow may be made out of a bag of muslin or dark denim and stuffed with a sweater or extra clothing. Much better – take a small pillow with you with removable and washable 'case' made of dark green or brown denim.

Kitchen Ware

In purchasing kitchen ware, a mistake is frequently made by getting a cheap kind of ware unfitted for the hard usage of camp life. The kind manufactured for hotels and restaurants and of sufficient capacity, is more expensive, but will outwear two outfits of the cheaper type and is really more economical in the long run. In the buying do not omit that most adaptable and convenient of all cooking utensils for camp – a wash boiler. Get one that is copper-lined and made of the heaviest tin.

Table Ware

Campers prefer the white enamel ware on account of its appearance and wear. If the imported kind is purchased it will last for at least three long-term seasons. Avoid tin and the cheap grey enamel ware. Each boy should be provided with a large plate of the deep soup pattern, cereal bowl not too large, a saucer for sauce and dessert, a cup, knife, fork, table spoon and tea spoon. In a small camp the boy usually brings his own 'eating utensils.' When the table is set with white oil cloth, white enamelled dishes, both serving and individual, with decorations of ferns, wild flowers or blossoms, the food always seems to taste better and the meal proceeds with that keen enjoyment, which is not only conducive to good digestion but promotive of good fellowship. A dirty table and dishes and rough-house table manners are a disgrace to a camp even as small as six boys. Cleanliness, courtesy and cheerful conversation contribute to the making of character while at meals.

Table Tops

Table tops should be made of matched boards and battened. Screw the battens[2] to the boards. The tables should be thirty-six inches in width. The length must be determined by the number of persons to be seated. The seating of boys in tent groups is considered the best plan.

A 'Horse' Idea

A wooden horse made after the following sketch will support the table top and seats. The seat may be a plank about twelve inches wide and one and one-eighth inches thick.

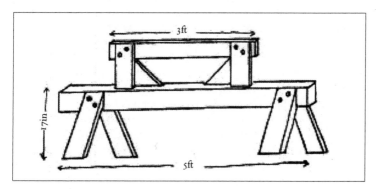

Wooden horse table and seat support

Buildings

Permanent buildings are largely planned according to the ideas of the director or organisation operating the camp and this, therefore, is a matter which cannot be fully treated in a book of this character. Convenience, harmony with natural surroundings, and adaptability are the three things which govern the planning and erection of permanent camp buildings. *Wilderness Homes* by Oliver Kemp, contains many suggestions for camps of this character. In *Recreation* for April 1911, is an excellent article by William D. Brinckle on 'Log Cabins'.

Surveying

The following practical suggestions on surveying in a boys' camp have been especially prepared by H.M. Allen. Surveying is an important subject for study and practice, as it is both interesting and useful and may serve as a stepping-stone in the later education of the boy.

The surveying may be roughly divided into two parts, simple and advanced. The simple work includes that which can be carried on with a few cheap instruments easily secured or made by the boys. The advanced work requires better instruments and is adapted to high school boys. Only the simple work will be described.

Home-made

The instruments needed in simple surveying are: compass, measuring tape, draughtsman's scale, protractor, drawing materials and a small home-made transit. The leader should, if possible, become familiar with some good textbook on surveying, such as Wentworth's *Plane Trigonometry and Surveying*. He should also get some civil engineer to give him a little instruction in the rudiments. It is well also to get some practice before going to camp. Any vacant lot or gymnasium floor will be suitable. If the leader is near a small lake that will be especially desirable.

The transit is easily made. A flat board should be selected, about twelve inches in diameter, which will not warp. Upon this a circle is marked about ten inches in diameter. For this purpose use a pair of drawing compasses. Then with a protractor lay off the degrees of the circle. A good plan is to mark the circle on bristol board[3] which can be tacked in the board. Then a pointed piece of wood ten inches long should be fastened with a nail in the centre of the circle. At the ends of the pointer, pins should be placed vertically so that they are in line with the pivot nail. This will form a sight for measuring the angles. The board is then mounted upon a pointed stick or tripod. You will need a hatchet and a half dozen sharpened sticks for markers. You are now ready for the survey.

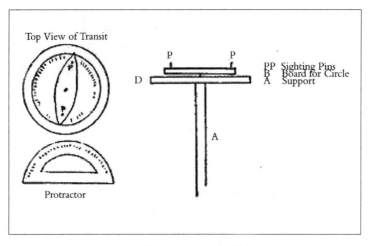

Top view of transit, protractor, sighting pins, board for circle, support

Camp Survey

To make a map of the location of the camp, the first thing is to locate a base line on a level piece of ground. At the two ends A and B stakes are placed and the length carefully measured with the tape. Then from one end of the line stretch a string about ten feet long, toward the other stake. Under this string place the compass. In this way the direction of the line may be learned.

In figure 1 above, the base line runs about 10 degrees west of north. Drive a stake where the tent is to be located. This place will be called C. Then place the transit at A and measure the angle formed by the imaginary lines AC and AB. In the example the angle is about 45 degrees. Then place the transit at B and measure the angle there, formed by the lines AB and BC. Then the angle at C should be measured and the sum of the angles thus measured will be 180 degrees, if the work is correct.

Now make a drawing of the survey. Draw on paper a line corresponding to the line AB, making a certain scale, say 100 feet to the inch. If the real line is 200 feet long, the line on the paper will be 2 inches. With the protractor the angles at B and A may be drawn or plotted. This will give the location of the point C. With the scale determine on the plan the length of the other sides of the triangle ABC. The actual distances should next be measured with the tape to test the accuracy of the survey.

Next place a stake along the side of the lake at a point D. Then in a similar manner measure the triangle with the transit. With the protractor the lines AD and BD can be plotted on the plan. With the scale the length of

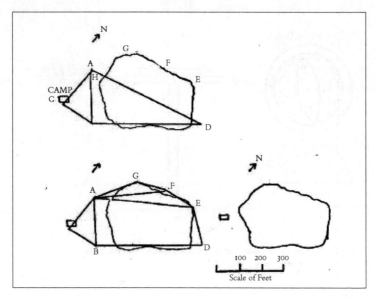

Fig. 2, fig. 3, fig. 4

the lines AD and BD can be estimated from the map. The rest of the lake is surveyed in the same manner. It is only necessary to take other points on the lake and survey the resulting triangles. It is a good idea to use four-foot stakes with flags placed so as to be easy to sight to them.

Finally a tracing may be made with carbon paper giving only the shore line and leaving out the lines of the triangles and the map is finished. The boys in one camp surveyed a lake a mile long with home-made instruments with excellent results.

Boys should be taught how to use the compass and a map in tracing their way through an unknown country. Also to travel by the stars or by the moss on the trees.

5

Personal Check List or Inventory

Experience only can determine what should be taken to camp. Usually the first camping trip decides what to take on the second trip, and also reveals how few things, providing they are right things, one really needs to be comfortable in camp. A boy's mother, who is generally the official trunk packer of the family, makes a mistake in stowing away in the trunk a lot of things not serviceable or suitable for camping. Cotton goods, except towels, handkerchiefs, and hose, are of no use. Grey woollen shirts, grey, brown, or green sweaters (a boon to campers – avoid white, red, or striped colours), khaki suit, outing flannel pyjamas (tan colour preferred) are in the class of real camp necessities so far as clothing is concerned. The hat should be drab or khaki colour, of campaign style, something that will shed water and sun.

The outfit may be divided into four classes: things necessary, things desirable, things convenient, and luxuries. Boys who go camping for two weeks or less should take articles in the following list marked (1); those who go for four weeks or less should take articles marked (2) in addition to those marked (1); and those who go for what may be called the season, six or more weeks, should take those marked (3), in addition to all of (1) and (2).

Necessary

Woollen sweater (coat style) (1)
Note book or diary (1)
Twine and rope (2)
Two flannel shirts (grey) (1)
Lead pencil (1)
Change of underwear (1)
Pens and ink (2)
Two pairs stockings (1)
Stamps, stamped envelopes (1)
Jersey (2)
Outing flannel pyjamas (1)
Paper, postals and envelopes (2)
Running trousers (1)
Handkerchiefs (1)

Needles and thread (1)
Two pairs woollen blankets (1)
Matches in metal box (1)
Poncho (1)
Folding drinking cup (1)
Turkish towels (1)
Strong pocket knife on chain (1)
Extra pair heavy shoes (2)
Toilet soap (in aluminium or celluloid box) (1)
Echo whistle (2)
Fishing tackle (2)
Comb and brush (1)
Camera (2)

Tooth brush and tooth paste (1)
Small-sized Bible (1)
Money (1)
Pins and safety pins (safeties one-inch
and four-inch) (1)
Good disposition (1)
Leggings-tan, army style (1)

Desirable

Extra suit of clothes (2)
Rubber-soled shoes (1)
Soft laundered shirt (2)
Bathing suit or tights (2)
Small compass (2)
Small mirror (1)
Whisk broom (2)
Tennis racquets and balls (3)
Dish towels (2)

Ping Pong racquets, balls (3)
Cheap watch (1)
Rubber boots or overshoes (2)
Map of vicinity (2)
Clothes pins (2)
Musical instruments (2)
Flash lamp (2)
Scissors (2)
Repair outfit (2)

Convenient

Games (3)
Can opener (2)
Books (3)
Small hand washboard (3)
Small pillow (2)

Thick strong gloves (3)
Mosquito netting (2)
Heavy woollen stockings (3)
Candles (3)
Elk hide moccasins (3)

Luxuries

Bath robe (3)
Blacking and brush (3)
Shaving outfit (3)

Laundry bag (2)
Face rag (3)

It is understood that cooking utensils, tools, tents, cots and the general camp equipment is supplied by the camp management. The above list is for the individual campers.

Mark Everything

Mark everything with your initials, or, if in a large camp, your camp number. This may be done with indelible ink upon white tape, and the tape sewed upon the garments, or you may order through the large department stores your full name embroidered on tape in sufficient quantity to sew upon your belongings. Marking your 'goods and chattels' helps identify ownership, for things somehow get fearfully mixed up in a boys' camp.

A clever scheme for locating lost articles was adopted by one large camp. A 'Lost and Found' shop was opened. Articles found were brought to the shop. Hours for identification and reclaiming were announced, the owner paying two cents for each article claimed. This method had the effect of making the boys more systematic and less careless in throwing things around, or leaving them upon the ground after a ball game or play. After a certain length of time, an auction was held of all unclaimed articles. The money received was put into books for the camp library.

Write it Down

Make your 'check list' during the winter. Have an old box handy in which to put things you think you will want to take to camp. Boys usually talk over the experiences of the last camp until about 1 January, then they begin to talk and plan about the next camp. As you think of things jot them down in a little memorandum book marked 'Camp Ideas'. Leaders will find this plan especially helpful. In making up the list, put down each article on a separate line. Don't jumble things together. Leave nothing to memory which, alas, too frequently is a splendid 'forgetter'. Write it down on paper. Examine your list very carefully, and strike out everything you can do without. Simplicity coupled with comfort should be the guide in making up the list or inventory. Pin the list on the inside of your trunk or camp box. Often the little trifles prove the most valuable things on a camping trip. For instance, a supply of giant safety pins is invaluable for pinning blankets together in sleeping-bag fashion. Ever roll out of your blankets or toss them off on a cool night? If so, you know the value of a giant safety pin.

What to pack the outfit in and how to pack it is a problem which each must solve for himself. A cracker box, with hinged cover, padlock, and rope handles, is good for a short-time camping trip. It should be of the following dimensions: 30 x 18 x 15 inches.

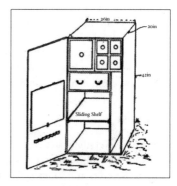

Camp box

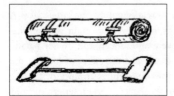

Blanket roll

A good strong steamer trunk is about the best thing. It is convenient, easy to handle, and takes up very little space.

The boys who are mechanically inclined, will want to have the fun of making a camp box. The illustration on page 41 is a suggestion successfully worked out by a number of boys. The dimensions may be determined by the maker. Don't make it too big, or it will be a burden and also occupy too much room in the tent. It stands upright and serves as a dresser. Boys who spend a summer in camp should have either a steamer trunk or this dresser.

If the trunk or box is too small to carry blankets, a good plan is to roll blankets, bedding and such articles in a roll or canvas, the ends and sides of which are doubled inward, so as to prevent articles from dropping out or getting wet. Strap with a good shawl or strong rope. (See illustration above.)

A dunnage,[1] duffle, or carry-all bag is sometimes used for packing, but there is a possibility of a 'mess' as well as a loss of your good disposition and patience in trying to locate some desired article.

Carry your poncho to be used in case of rain en route.

Shipping

Have your express man deliver your baggage at the station at least one hour before the train starts. If the baggage is delayed, much annoyance and loss of temper is the result. If the camp is a large one, some one should be designated to look after the baggage arrangements. After checking the baggage, this person should receive checks and attend to claiming baggage at destination.

Many of the large camps provide mucilaged labels or 'stickers' to paste on the end of the trunk or box making identification easy at railroad baggage room. Initials and camp number should be painted on outside of trunk or box.

Neatness

'A place for everything and everything in place' should be the real key to find things in your trunk. Neatness is good discipline for the mind, and should characterise every real camper. The trunks of some boys in camp look as if a cyclone had struck them. 'Full, pressed down, and running over.' Every old thing in any old way is both slovenly and unhygienic.

About once a week everything should be taken from the trunk or box, and exposed to the sun. Let the sun also get into the trunk or box. Then repack neatly. This will prevent mould and dampness, and be the means of discovering lost articles. Finally be sure to go over with care your 'check list' or inventory the day before camp breaks. This will prevent rushing around excitedly at the eleventh hour, hunting lost articles.

General Hints

Grey and khaki are the most inconspicuous colours for camping.

Shirts should be provided with breast pockets.

Each lock should have a duplicate key to be given to the tent leader, or in a large camp, to the camp banker.

Have an old laundry bag in which to put soiled clothes. 'Wash day' is a popular day in many camps. No camper need be dirty when there is abundance of water.

There is a luxuriance in a piece of soap and a clean towel that only experienced campers can understand and appreciate.

Wet towels, swimming suits or tights should not be placed in the trunk or box, but hung upon a rope, or non-rust wire outside of the tent.

The poncho is the camper's friend. It makes a good rubber blanket, a wrap, a cushion, a bag, a sail or a tent.

Be sure to take enough bed clothes. You will need them on cold nights.

Stamps wiped over the hair of your head will not stick together – the oil of the hair does the trick. Take a self-filler fountain pen – no glass filler to break.

A small Williams or Colgate shaving stick box, with screw or hinged cover, makes a good match box. A better one is a water-tight hard rubber box, with screw top. If dropped into a lake or stream it will float, whereas a metal box will sink.

Some one has said that 'Good temper is as necessary for camping as water is for swimming.' Be sure it is on your 'check list.'

6

Organisation, Administration and Discipline

The heavens themselves, the planets and this centre
Observe degree, priority and place,
Insisture, course, proportion, season, form,
Office and custom, in all lines of order.

(*Troilus and Cressida*. Act 1, Scene 3)

Order

It matters very little if the camp be a large or small one, all will agree that system and organisation must prevail if the camp is to be a 'place of known delight and proved desire.' Order is said to be Heaven's first law, and a boys' camp should not be operated contrary to this recognised law. What is everybody's business usually becomes nobody's business. Much soup has been spoiled by the stirring of too many cooks. A boys' camp becomes a place of discord when everybody takes a hand in 'running it'. There must be one whose word is absolute and final, and who is recognised as the leader or director of the camp; at the same time the campers should have a voice in the government and share in planning and participating in its activities. (See chapter on Leadership).

The following charting of organisation will explain the 'degree, priority and place' of those who are to be responsible for the administration and welfare of the camp.

Cooperative Self-Government

This form of organisation recognises maturity, experience, ability, cooperation, justice and altruistic service. Self-government wholly by the boys is unwise. There must always be a paternal guidance of hot, impulsive and indiscriminate youth. Boys desire adult leadership and where a wise combination is formed of man and boy working together, there will be found the highest type of efficient, wholesome, happy and purposeful camp life.

Council Meetings

Frequent council meetings should be held. When the senior council, composed of the leaders and director, meet for planning and to discuss the work, it should be understood that whatever is said or discussed at the meeting, must not be talked over in the presence of the boys, particularly matters of discipline, awarding of honours and camp policy. Joint meetings of the junior and senior councils should be held weekly. Each 'tent' is represented on the junior council by electing one of their tent-mates, who shall present the views of his constituents at council meetings.

Departments

The director should have the power of appointing the chairmen or heads of departments; and the chairmen the privilege of selecting associates from the two councils. The policy of each department must be ratified by a joint meeting of the councils before it becomes operative. Prevent bickering over minor parliamentary details. Keep in mind first, last and always, the highest welfare of the camp. Let the 'voice of the people' be heard, yet see that the legislation introduced is in the interest of the highest good of the campers. The chart suggests the work of the various departments.

Rules

In all well-organised and purposeful camps for boys, three rules are considered absolutely essential for the safety and welfare of the campers. These rules are:

1 No fire-arms, air-rifles or explosives of any kind allowed.
2 No one of the party shall enter the water for swimming or bathing, except during the designated period.
3 No tobacco used in any form.

Every boy going to camp agrees, in signing his application, to observe whatever rules are decided upon as best for the welfare of all. Boys should be trusted and expected to do as the majority think best. There should be a happy understanding and mutual confidence existing which should make a long list of rules unnecessary. When the boys arrive in camp, the director should outline and explain the purpose and policy of the camp in kind, but unmistakable terms.

A camp of a dozen boys and their school teacher, was operated for three delightful weeks, upon the following 'agreement', which all the boys and their leader signed.

We, the members of Camp Bejoyful, do hereby subscribe cheerfully to the following rules and regulations and will be governed by them while we are members of this camp.

We further agree to pay any penalty the other members of the camp may think fit to impose upon us for breaking these rules or resolutions.

We will not lose our tempers.

We will not use any language we would not use in the presence of ladies.

We will not tell stories we would not tell or want told to our sisters.

We will perform cheerfully any duties our Camp Master asks us to perform.

We will at all times respect the rights and feelings of others.

We will remember that the command to 'Remember the Sabbath day and keep it holy,' is obligatory at all times and in all places.

The motto of this camp shall be 'Noblesse oblige.'

The Whistle

Unless the camp is conducted under the auspices of the Boys' Brigade or some military organisation, where boys prefer the military discipline, it is unwise to introduce it in a camp for boys. The type of discipline to be used will depend upon the type of leader. Some camps are controlled by the use of a whistle. When the attention of the boys is desired, the leader blows a shrill blast of the whistle and the boys immediately respond by absolute silence and await the announcement or whatever the leader or director desires to say to them. Never blow the whistle unless necessary. Secure first the attention of the boys if you want their interest. Camp boys become accustomed to continuous blowing of the whistle in the same manner that city boys become used to the noise of the street-car gong. Blow your whistle and wait. Cause for a second blast should be considered serious.

Conscience

In a camp where through the thoughtlessness of a boy a misdemeanour had been committed, the leader explained at the camp fire how mean the action was and said that he did not believe there was a boy in camp who, if he had realised its contemptible nature, would for one moment have thought of doing such a thing. He concluded his remarks by saying, 'If there is any boy here who knows who did this thing, I earnestly request that he will keep it to himself and not breathe the name of the offender to anyone in camp.' Especially did he request that on no account should the offender's name be told to him. There were a few rather red faces about the camp fire, but the name of the offender was never known and no similar misdemeanour occurred while the camp was open.

Self-Imposed Discipline

In another camp two boys had thoughtlessly violated the understanding regarding swimming and they spent an hour on the hillside with the leader discussing the situation. After the leader had explained to them his responsibility to the parents of each boy in camp and how insecure parents would feel if they thought their boys were not being properly taken care of, he asked them: 'Now, if you were in my place, what would you do with two such fellows?' And they both replied that they thought the two boys should be sent home as an example to the rest of the camp. The leader agreed with them and the two boys, who had pronounced their own sentence, left the next morning for home. That leader has today no better friends among boys than those two particular fellows.[1]

Seven Things Which God Hates

Solomon in his book of Proverbs says,

> These six things does the Lord hate: yea, seven are an abomination unto him. A proud look, a lying tongue, and hands that shed innocent blood, a heart that deviseth wicked imaginations, feet that be swift in running to mischief, a false witness that speaketh lies, and he that soweth discord among brethren. (Proverbs; 16:19)

Liars and Sneaks

Punish the liar heavily. Help the boy to see that to make a mistake and own up to it, is regarded in a much more favourable light than to sneak and lie out of it. Have him understand that the lie is the worst part of the offence. It is awful to have the reputation of being a liar, for even when a boy does tell the truth nobody believes him because of his past reputation. Never indulge suspicion. Above all discountenance sneaking; nothing is more harmful than to maintain a feeble discipline through the medium of tale-bearing.

Never keep a boy in camp who is out of tune with the camp life or its standards, and whose presence only serves to militate against the real purpose of the camp. 'Grouchitis' is a catching disease.

Meditation Log

The methods of punishment are as varied as the colours of the rainbow. In one camp, a 'Meditation Log,' upon which the boy sits and thinks, and thinks, and thinks, and – . No doubt he is a sadder and wiser boy for his period of meditation. A 'wood pile' where boys saw from one to five or more sticks of cord wood into stove lengths, is an economic mode of punishment, for it not only provides wood for the kitchen stove, but hardens the boys' muscle as well as helps him to remember his mistakes and to avoid repetition. Walking around the campus for a certain length of time carrying an oar over the shoulder, is another method. Curtailing a boy's privileges, such as swimming, boating, taking away his dessert, are other methods in vogue in boys' camps. When a boy swears, if he is a 'scout,' the other 'scouts' pour a cup of cold water down the offender's sleeve or back, for each offence. Some boys have been cured of swearing by having their mouths washed out with 'Welcome Soap', publicly, along the shore of the lake or stream, with camp-mates as silent spectators. Make the 'punishment fit the crime,' but always the kind of punishment which the boy will acknowledge is deserved and just. Never punish in anger.

Private Talks

A 'heart-to-heart' talk with the boy during a walk in the woods, or in some quiet place of the camp, will do more good to get him to see and realise his need of adjustment to camp life and enlist his willingness to try again and to 'do his best' than any form of physical punishment.

When it becomes necessary to send a boy home, always telegraph or write his parents, telling them on what train or boat they may expect him and the reason for sending him home.

7

The Day's Programme

A Morning Prayer

The day returns and brings in the petty round of irritating concerns and duties. Help us to play the man, help us to perform them with laughter and kind faces. Let cheerfulness abound with industry. Give us to go blithely on our business all the day. Bring us to our resting beds weary and content and undishonored, and grant us in the end the gift of sleep.

(Robert Louis Stevenson)

Requisites

All the major habits of life are formed during the teen period of life. If camping teaches a boy anything it teaches him the habit of being systematic. The day's programme should be built upon a platform calculated not only to keep the camp running smoothly, but to develop within the boy and man those qualities requisite for a good camper, viz., truth, sincerity, self-control, courage, energy, skill, mental capacity, justice, patriotism, stamina, efficiency, executive power, consideration, kindliness, cheerfulness, self-reliance, good temper, good manners, tact, promptness, obedience, helpfulness, and cooperation. Camping has as good an effect on a boy's character as it has upon his health. It teaches him to be self-reliant, to look after his own wants, and not to be abnormally self-centred. It is marvellous how much more tidy and considerate a boy becomes after he has had a season in camp, looking after himself and his own belongings, as well as sharing in keeping his tent neat and clean, and having his part in the day's work. From 'reveille' at 7 a.m. to 'taps' at 9 p.m. the day's programme should be definitely planned. In order to make this chapter of practical value the different periods of the day and its activities will be described very fully and enough suggestions given to make the day purposeful, educational, recreational and attractive in either a large or small camp.

7 a.m. is usually the hour of beginning the day, although some camps make the rising hour 6.30 a.m. The first morning in camp boys want to get up around 4 a.m., thinking it about three hours later, on account of the sun streaming into their tent. After the first morning boys who wake early should be expected

to keep silent and remain in their tent until 'reveille' sounds. Consideration should be shown toward those who desire to sleep.

7.00

When the bugle sounds 'reveille' everybody turns out in pyjamas or swimming tights and indulges in a brisk ten-minute setting-up exercise. This should be made snappy, giving particular attention to correcting stooping shoulders and breathing. Boys should not be excused from this exercise unless ill. At the end of the exercise the flag is raised and the campers salute the Union Jack as they are flung to the morning breeze. A small cannon is fired in some camps when the flag is raised. The honour of raising the flag may be given to the boys of the tent having won the honour tent pennant of the preceding day or to boys specially assigned. The spirit of patriotism is fostered by respect to the flag.

7.15

Flag-raising is followed by a dip in the lake. It should be understood that this is to be a dip or plunge and not a swim. Five minutes is sufficient time to be in the water. Place some responsible person in charge of the dip. A safe rule is never to permit boys in the water unless supervised. The boys should take soap, towels and tooth brushes with them when they go for the dip. A good morning scrub of the teeth with a brush saves many hours of pain. Boys are woefully negligent (because ignorant) of the care of their teeth. Saturday is 'scrub' day in many of the large camps when all are required to take a 'soap scrub.' Marvellous how the 'tan' disappears after this scrubbing period!

7.30

By this time every fellow is hungry enough to devour whatever food is set before him, whether he is fond of it or not, and there is an alacrity of response to the Mess Call of the bugle which only a camper understands and appreciates. When the campers are seated there is either silent or audible grace before the meal is eaten. Take plenty of time for the eating of the meal. Forty-five minutes is not too long. Encourage wholesome conversation and good natural pleasantry, but discountenance 'rough house' and ungentlemanliness. The announcements for the day are usually given at the breakfast table followed by the reading of a chapter from the Bible and a short prayer.

8.30

A boy should be taught that all labour is noble, that 'no one can rise that slights his work' and the 'grand business in life is not to see what lies dimly at a distance, but to do what lies clearly at hand.' With this kind of a spirit, blankets are taken out of the tent to be aired and the sides of the tent tied up, the camp is cleaned and put in a sanitary condition, the tents are put in order, and kitchen work, if part of the boys' duties, is attended to. All work should be finished by 9.30. Labour of some sort should be a part of his daily life while at camp, for when one gets to love work, his life becomes a happy one. The world despises a shirker but honours a worker.

The work of the day is sometimes done by tent groups or by boys grouped in alphabetical order, each group being under a leader whose part is assigned daily by the Camp Director (see chapter on Organisation). In the writer's camp, work is considered a great privilege. For instance, if three bushels of peas must be picked from the camp garden for dinner, a call is made for volunteers. From forty to fifty hands will go up and after careful choosing, six boys are selected to do this coveted work, much to the disappointment of the others. It is all in the way work is presented to the boys, whether they will look upon it as a privilege or an irksome task.

9.30 to 11.00

If tutoring is a part of the camp's plan, the morning will be found a desirable time for tutor and boy to spend an hour together. Manual training, instruction in woodcraft, field and track athletics, boating, life-saving drills, rehearsal for shows or entertainments, photography, tennis, cricket, are some of the many activities to be engaged in during this period. One day a week, each box or trunk should be aired, and its contents gone over carefully. A sort of 'clean up' day.

11.00

About this time the Life Saving Crew will be getting ready for their drill and patrolling of the swim. The other campers will be taking in their blankets and after shaking them well and folding, will place them on their beds for the inspection, which usually comes at noon. At 11.20 boys who cannot swim should be given instruction by those who can swim. If this is done before the regular swim there is less danger and greater progress is made.

11.30

This seems to be the popular hour for swimming in nearly all the camps. It follows the cricket game, the tennis match, the camp work, and usually the temperature of air and water is just right for a swim. Allow no swimmer to go beyond the line of patrol boats. Have some one on shore who is keen to observe any boy who may be in need of assistance.

Twenty minutes is sufficient length of time to be in fresh water. When the boys come out of the water, have a towel drill, teaching the boy how to use the towel so that his back may be dried as well as every other part of his body. This rubbing down induces circulation of the blood and gives that finish to a swim which makes the boy feel like a new being. It is unwise to permit boys to lie around undressed after a swim, for physiological as well as moral reasons. Swimming tights should be wrung out dry, either by hand or by a wringer kept near the swimming place, and hung out on a rope or rustless wire, stretched back of the tent. Do not permit wet clothes to be hung in the tent, on the canvas or tent ropes.

12.00

Beds or bunks should be made up for inspection. Three men or boys may be appointed as inspectors. Considerable interest and pride is taken by the boys in having their canvas home look neat. This training in neatness, order and cleanliness is invaluable. (See chapter on Awards). The inspection should not take over twenty minutes. While this is going on those who have kitchen or table duty will be busily engaged getting tables in readiness for dinner.

12.30

Mess call for dinner. This meal should be the heartiest meal of the day, and plenty of time given to the eating of the food. Mail is usually given out at this meal in camps where there is but one delivery a day.

1.15, 'Siesta'

'Siesta,' or rest hour, follows dinner. In the early days of boys' camps this suggestion would have been laughed at, but today it is looked upon as highly hygienic and considered one of the best things of camp and strongly to be commended. The boy is advised to lie down flat on his back, in his tent or under the shade of a friendly tree, and be quiet. He may talk if he wishes, but usually some one reads aloud to his fellows. This gives the food a chance to digest, and the whole body a nerve and muscle rest before the active work of the afternoon.

2.00 to 4.30

These hours will be spent in various ways. Usually it is the time for athletic sports, baseball games, quoit[1] tournaments, tennis tournaments, excursions afield, boat regatta, archery, water sports, scouting games and other activities in which most of the campers can engage. The big outdoor events should occupy this time of the day.

4.30

Where daily inspection is a part of the camp plan the boys will begin getting everything in readiness for that important event. A general bustle of activity will be in evidence and every boy on the *qui vive*[2] to have his tent win the coveted honour pennant, usually given for the neatest tent.

5.00

Inspection is conducted during the absence of the boys. While the inspectors are making the round of tents, the boys should assemble either in the permanent building of the camp or under some big tree, to listen to a practical talk by the camp physician, a demonstration in first aid work, the reading of a story, or to something equally educational in character. This is a valuable hour when occupied in this manner. (See chapter on inspection, awards, etc.)

6.00

Supper hour cannot come too promptly for active boys. The announcement of the day's inspection should be made at the meal and the honour pennant or flag presented to the successful tent, and accepted by one of the boys. This occasion is usually a time of rejoicing, also a time of resolve-making on the part of tent groups to 'do better tomorrow.' The record of each tent is read by one of the inspectors, and at the end of the week the tent having the best record gets a special supper or 'seconds' on ice cream day.

6.45

About this time, with the going down of the sun, nature seems to quiet down, and it is the psychological time for serious thought. Many camps devote twenty minutes to Bible study (for suggested lessons, see chapter on Religion and Moral Life). Tent groups under their leader study thoughtfully the meaning of life and the great lessons taught by God through nature. Night after night the boys consciously or unconsciously acquire through this study the requisites of a good camper mentioned in the first part of this chapter.

7.15

Campus games, boating, preparation for the bonfire, etc., will occupy the time until dark. Every boy should be engaged in some recreational play, working off whatever surplus energy he may have at hand so that when the time for 'turning in' comes, he will be physically tired and ready for bed.

8.00

The evening programme varies. Some nights there will be a show, other nights a camp fire, or mock trial, an illustrated talk, or 'village school entertainment,' or a play, or a musical evening or 'vo-de-ville.' Leave about two nights a week open. The boys prefer to have occasional open evenings when they are free to loaf around, and go to bed early. Plan the evening 'stunts' very carefully.

8.45

The bugler blows 'tattoo'[1] which means 'all in tents.' After the boys have undressed and are ready for bed, the leader reads a chapter from the Bible, and in many camps the boys lead in volunteer prayer, remembering especially the folks at home.

From a hill near camp, or from a boat on the lake come the notes of a familiar hymn such as 'Abide With Me,' 'Lead, Kindly Light,' 'The Day is Past and Over,' 'Sun of My Soul,' or 'Nearer, My God to Thee,' played by the bugler. Every boy listens and the ear records a suggestion which helps to make the night's sleep pure and restful. Try it. Taps played slowly, follows the hymn. As the last notes are being echoed upon the still night air the lights are being extinguished in the tents, so that when the final prolonged note ends the camp is in darkness and quiet, and all have entered into a nine-hour period of restoration of body and mind. Who knows, but God himself, how many of the boys, and even leaders, while wrapped warmly in their blankets have silently breathed out that old, old prayer so full of faith, which has been handed down from generation to generation:

Now I lay me down to sleep
I pray Thee Lord my soul to keep.

A prayer echoed by the camp director, for now is the only time of the day's programme when he begins to breathe freely, and is partially able to lay aside his mantle of responsibility. A cough, a sigh, and even the moaning of the wind disturbs this ever vigilant leader and he thinks of his charges, until finally, weariness conquers and sleep comes.

The Well-Ordered Day

How shall the day be ordered? To the sage The young man spoke. And this was his reply:

A morning prayer.
A moment with thy God who sends thee dawn
Up from the east; to thank heaven for the care
That kept thee through the night; to give thy soul,
With faith serene, to his complete control;
To ask his guidance still along the way.
    So starts the day.

A busy day.
Do with a will the task that lies before.
So much there is for every man to do,
And soon the night when man can work no more.
And none but he to life's behest is true

Who works with zeal and pauses only when
He stretches forth his hand to help the men
Who fail or fall beside him on the way.
    So runs the day.

A merry evening.
When toil is done, then banished be the care
That frets the soul. With loved ones by the hearth
The evening hour belongs to joy and mirth;
To lighter things that make life fresh and fair.
For honest work has earned its hour of play.
    So ends the day.

                    (John Clair Minot in the *Independent*)

Bibliography

'Association Boys' Camps' – Edgar M. Robinson. *Association Boys*, Vol. I., No.3, 1902.

'The Day's Program' – C. Hanford Henderson. *How to Help Boys*, Vol. III., No.3, 1903.

The Camp Conference, *Secretary's Report*, 1905–06 (out of print).

The Camp Conference, *How to Help Boys*, July 1903.

8

Moral and Religious Life

> The aspect of nature is devout. Like the figure of Jesus, she stands with bended head and hands folded upon her breast.
>
> (Emerson)

Camp life should help boys to grow not only physically and mentally, but morally. Religion is the basis of morality. The highest instinct in man is the religious. Man made the city with all its artificiality, but, as some one has said, 'God made the country.' Everything that the city boy comes in contact with is man made.

> Even the ground is covered with buildings and paving blocks; the trees are set in rows like telegraph poles; the sunlight is diluted with smoke from the factory chimneys, the moon and stars are blotted out by the glare of the electric light; and even the so-called lake in the park is a scooped-out basin filled by pumps. Little wonder that a boy who grows up under these conditions has little reverence for a God whose handiwork he has not seen.[1]

Nature's Teachings

> When a boy's soul is open to the influence of nature he feels the presence of the divine in the forest. There is an uplift, an inspiration, a joy that he never experiences in the city. He does not know how to express himself, but somehow he feels the spiritual atmosphere pervading the woods which his soul breathes in as really as his nostrils do the pure air, and he is ready to Go forth, under the open sky and list to Nature's teachings.
>
> (Bryant)

For as Martin Luther said, 'God writes the Gospel not in the Bible alone, but in trees and flowers and clouds and stars.'

Sunday

Sunday in a boys' camp should be observed by the holding of a service in the morning, with song, scripture reading, prayer and a short talk. The afternoon is usually occupied by letter writing, Bible study, or reading, the day closing with a vesper service in the evening just as the sun is setting. Boisterousness should not be encouraged. Unnatural restraint, however, is contrary to the spirit of the day. The day should be different from other days. Many camp boys date their first real awakening to the best and highest things in life from a Sunday spent in camp.

Every real camper has experienced a Sunday similar to this one described by Howard Henderson:

A quiet Sunday in the deep woods is a golden day to be remembered for many a year. All nature combines to assist the camper in directing his thoughts to the great Author of all the beauty that he beholds. 'The heavens declare the glory of God; and the firmament sheweth his handiwork.' The trees under which one reclines rear their heads heavenward, pointing their spire-like minarets far up toward the blue-vaulted roof. It inspires the very soul to worship in these unbuilt cathedrals with wilderness of aisle and pillars, which for elegance and beauty have never been equalled by the architects of any age. And the music of the trees combined with the notes of the bird songsters, give a joy which is unknown in listening to a city choir.

Bible Study

The Bible becomes a new book to boys when studied under such an environment. As one boy wrote home to his father after a Sunday spent in a camp where Sunday was observed in this manner, 'Dad, it is so different here, from a Sunday at home; I understood the talk and the Bible study was great; it was a bully day!'

The following Bible course was worked out by the author and has been used in scores of boys' camps. These lessons were taught to groups of boys at eventide when nature seemed to quiet down and the boys were most responsive to good, sensible suggestion. The camp was divided into tent groups, each group being taught by their leader or an exchange leader, one group occupying a big rock, another the 'Crow's Nest,' or 'Tree House,' another getting together under a big tree, another in their tent. No leader was permitted to take more than twenty minutes for the lesson. It is unwise to take twenty minutes for what could be said in ten minutes. The boys all had a chance to take part in the discussion. Each lesson was opened and closed with prayer, many of the boys participating in volunteer prayer. In teaching a lesson don't spend too much time in description unless you have the rare gift of being able to make your scene live before your hearers. Talk plainly and to the point. Naturalness should characterise each lesson. Boys hate cant[2] and apologies and lack of definiteness. Your best illustrations will be drawn from the life of the camp and from nature.

In some camps these lessons were taught in the morning directly after breakfast, while the boys were seated at the tables.

There are 'Sermons in stones, and good in every thing,' therefore the purpose of these lessons should be to help boys hear these sermons and learn nature's lessons of purity, strength and character.

A course in bible study

Lesson 1. The hills-prayer
Psalm 121.
Christ going into the mountains to pray.
Matt. 14:23; Mark 6:46; Luke 6:12; Mark 1:35; Matt. 6:6–15.

Practical thoughts:
Unnatural not to pray. Even Pagans pray, but they pray through fear.
More things are wrought through prayer than this world dreams of.

(Tennyson)

Pray to Christ as friend to friend. The Lord's Prayer.

He prayeth well who loveth well
Both man and bird and beast.
He prayeth best who loveth best
All things both great and small,
For the dear God who loveth us
He made and loveth all.

(Coleridge's 'Ancient Mariner')

Strength received through prayer. A time and place for prayer.

Lesson 2. The Birds – Dependence Upon God
Matt. 6:26; Psa.147:9; Luke 12:24; Matt. 10:29–31.

Practical thoughts:
God feeding the birds. How much more does God care for you. Not one forgotten, the most worthless, the most restless.
God loves the birds. He loves you. Show your love to Him by caring for the birds.

Isa. 40: 28–31.
Abraham Lincoln and the bird fallen from the nest. – 'Gentlemen, I could not have slept tonight if I had not helped that little bird in its trouble, and put it back safe in the nest with its mother.'

Lesson 3. Flowers – purity

Matt. 6:28–30. Beauty of flowers.

Isa. 55:10–13. Provision for summer growth and beauty.

Practical thoughts:

(Bring wild flowers to the class.)

Flowers come up out of the dirt yet unsoiled.

Possible for boys to keep clean and pure, surrounded by evil.

Evil thoughts determine evil deeds.

'My strength is as the strength of ten because my heart is pure.'

(Sir Galahad)

Purity of character, the lily.

Know thyself. Keep thyself pure. 1 Cor. 3:16,17.

White Cross Pledge.

Virtue never dwelt long with filth and nastiness.

(Count Rumford)

Lesson 4. Trees – growth

Psalm 1. (Hold the session under the biggest and best proportioned tree.)

Practical thoughts:

Cedars of Lebanon – Strong in the Lord.

The oaks – From acorns grew.

The fruit tree – Living for others.

By their fruits ye shall know them.

Stunted trees. Crooked trees.

Scarred trees. Grafted trees.

Matt. 1:16–20; Jer. 11:7, 8.

Things that interfere with a boy's growth.

Lesson 5. Water-life

(Hold the session along the shore.)

Psa. 65:9–13. God's liberality.

Isa. 55: 1. Freeness of the gospel.

John 4:14. Woman at the well.

Rev. 22:11. The last invitation in the Bible.

Practical thoughts:

The joy of living. The fun at camp.

Friendship.

Temporal life vs. eternal life.
Water will only satisfy thirst temporarily.
Water revives – Christ satisfies.
Eternal life for the asking.

Lesson 6. Rocks – Character

(Hold the session on or near some big boulder or rock.)
Matt. 7:24–27. A good foundation.
1 Cor. 3:9–14.

Practical thoughts:
All boys are building character day by day.
All builders have a choice of foundation.
All foundations will be tried.
Only one foundation will stand.
Jesus Christ is the Rock of Ages.

Every thought that we've ever had
Its own little place has filled.
Every deed we have done, good or bad
Is a stone in the temple we build.

(Sargant)

Character, not reputation, will alone stand the final test.

Lesson 7. Storms – trouble

Matt. 8:23–27. Need of help.
Phil. 4:6. A strong deliverer.
Psa. 107:28–30. A safe place.

Practical thoughts:
Boys have real troubles, real temptations, real shipwrecks.
Difficulties in school life, at home, in camp.
Almost ready to give up.
Have faith in Christ as a Saviour.

The inner side of every cloud
Is bright and shining,
I therefore turn my clouds about,
And always wear them inside out
To show the lining.

'Look ever to Jesus. He'll carry you through.'

Lesson 8. Sports – mastery

(Teach this lesson after a field day.)

    1 Cor. 9:24–27. The race of life. Mastery of self.

    Heb. 12:1, 2. Run with patience.

    1 Tim. 6:12. A good fight.

    Rev. 2:10. Faithfulness.

    Ecele. 9:11. Not always to the swift.

    Eccle. 9:10. Wholeheartedness.

Practical thoughts:

'Each victory of self will help you some other to win.'

    Self-control.

    Value of training. You are either master or slave.

    The Bible, the book of instruction.

    Solomon's rule of self-defence. Prov. 15: 1.

Lesson 9. Night – sin

Psa. 19. Night unto night.

    John 3:19–20. Evil deeds.

    Rom. 13:11–14. Awake out of sin.

Practical thoughts:

    Bad thoughts come to us in the dark.

    Dark places productive of crime.

    Mischief at camp during the night.

    Darkness cannot hide us from God.

    'Thou God seest me.'

    North star a guide for sailors – Jesus Christ a safe guide.

    'Character is what a man is in the dark.' (D.L. Moody)

Lesson 10. Chums – friendship

1 Sam. 18:1–4. True friendship.

    1 John 4:11. Love one another.

    1 Cor. 13:4–7. To the end.

Practical thoughts:

Chum means 'to abide with,' to share the same tent. Camp chums. David and Jonathan. The genuine article. Helping each other. The Friend – Jesus Christ.

Lesson 11. Camp fires

Build a camp fire along the shore. Read alternately the twenty-first chapter of the gospel of St John. The fire on the beach. John 21:9.

Practical thoughts:
    Jesus was there – Jesus is here.
    Peter confessed Him there. John 21:15–17.
    Who will confess Him here?
    Peter denied Him by another fire. Luke 22:54–62.
    Will you deny Him here?
    P.S. Make this a decision meeting.

Lesson 12. Fishing – personal work

Luke 5:1-11. Fishers of men.

Practical thoughts:
    Sometimes fish are caught and used as bait to catch others. When a boy becomes a Christian he should bring to others the same blessing.

Patience is essential in fishing – same in winning boys to Christ. Every fisherman expects to catch fish. To lead others to Christ is the noblest work in the world. Dan. 12: 3.

    Tent Devotions
    In some camps a bit of Scripture is read each night in the tent just before retiring. The following readings having been prepared by W.H. Wones, C.C. Robinson, Arthur Wilson and Charles R. Scott. Just before taps, if you have a good cornetist, have him go a short distance from the camp and play a well known hymn, like 'Abide With Me,' 'Nearer, My God, to Thee,' 'Lead, Kindly Light,' then play 'taps.' The effect is wonderful, and prevents all inclination toward noise or 'rough house.'

July
Topic: vacation

1   Personal Work on a Journey. John 4:5–15.
2   Its Results. John 4:27–30, 39, 42.
3   The Disciples' Trip for Service. Mark 6:7–13.
4   Their Interrupted Vacation. Mark 6:30–42.
5   A Night on the Lake. Mark 6:45–56.
6   A Foolish Journey. Luke 15:11–17.
7   A Wise Return. Luke 15:18–24.
8   The Welcome Guest. John 12:1–9.
9   A Fishing Experience. John 21:1–14.

10 Spending a Night on a Mountain. Luke 9:28–36.

11 Vacation Suggestion: 'Keep Sweet.' Psalm 34:8–15.

12 Vacation Suggestion: 'Stick to Principle.' Psalm 119:25–32.

13 Vacation Suggestion: 'Confess Christ.'; Matthew 10:24-33.

14 Vacation Suggestion: 'Keep up Bible Study.'; Psalm 119:1–8.

15 Vacation Suggestion: 'Write Good Letters.' 1 Corinthians 16:3–13.

16 Speaking for Christ While Travelling; Acts 8:26–39.

17 A Queen's Visit. 1 Kings 10:1–10.

18 An Adventurous Voyage. Acts 27:1–13.

19 Shipwreck. Acts 27:14–26.

20 All Saved. Acts 27:27–44.

21 Praying for a Prosperous Journey. Romans 1:8–16.

22 A Traveller's Adventures. 2 Corinthians 11:23–33.

23 A Merry Heart Desirable. Proverbs 15:13–17.

24 Keeping from Sin. Romans 6:16–23.

25 Meeting a Stranger. Luke 24:13–27.

26 A Delightful Surprise. Luke 24:28–35.

27 Jacob's Bivouac. Genesis 28:10–22.

28 David's Prayer in the Cave. Psalm 142:1–7.

29 Avoiding Sinful Pleasure. Hebrews 11:23–27.

30 Peter's Counsel. 1 Peter 4:1–10.

31 The Greatest Pleasure. Psalm 16:1–11.

August
Topic: nature

1 The Story of Nature's Creation. Genesis 1:11–22.

2 The First Garden. Genesis 2:8–17.

3 God's Care for His Creation. Matthew 6:25–34.

4 The Symbol of Peace. Genesis 8:1–11.

5 The Sign of God's Promise. Genesis 9:8–17.

6 The Burning Bush. Exodus 3:1–6.

7 The Accompaniment of God's Presence. Exodus 19:16–25.

8 Nature Halts to Accomplish God's Purpose. Joshua 10:5–14.

9 Nature's Tribute to God's Glory. Psalm 97:1–12.

10 The Midnight Hymn. Psalm 8:1–9.

11 The Sunrise Hymn. Psalm 19:1–14.

12 The Thunder-storm Hymn. Psalm 29:1–11.

13 The God of Storm. Matthew 8:23–33.

14 Nature has no perils for the God-fearing Man. Job 5:8–27.

15 The Full Ear. Matthew 13:1–9, 18, 23.

16 Harmful Weeds. Matthew 13:24–30, 36–43.

17 The God of Nature Protects Us. Psalm 121:1–8.

18   He Cares for Us. Psalm 147:1–20.

19   God's Voice After the Storm. 1 Kings 19:5–13.

20   The Tree of Life. Proverbs 3:13–21.

21   The Trees Desire a King. Judges 9:8–15; Joshua 24:15.

22   The Root Out of Dry Ground. Isaiah 53:1–12.

23   Water Without Price. Isaiah 55:1–13.

24   The Perfect Vine. John 15:1–14.

25   The Light Brighter than the Sun. Acts 9:1–20.

26   A Wonderful Star. Matthew 2:1–11.

27   Sand or Rock? Matthew 7:24–27.

28   Broken Branches. Matthew 21:1–11.

29   The Unprofitable Tree. Matthew 7:15–21.

30   The Profitable Tree. Psalm 1:1–6.

31   Do Good in all Seasons. Ecclesiastes 3:1–12.

Boy Scout Course

For a Boy Scout Camp, the following course, 'Boy's Scout Guide Book Study,' was prepared by W.S. Dillon:

The scout's oath

Lesson 1. To Do My Duty to God and My Country. Daniel 1:8; 6:4–10.

Lesson 2. To Help Other People at All Times. Exodus 3:1–11.

Lesson 3. To Obey the Scout Law. Exodus 20:3–17; Luke 10:26, 27; Matthew 7:12.

The scout salute and sign

Lesson 4. Judges 12:6; Acts 4:12; Galatians 6:14.

Three classes of scouts the tenderfoot

Lesson 5. Luke 5:1–11.

The second class scout

Lesson 6. Have at Least One Month's Service as a Tenderfoot. 2 Samuel 15:1–6.

Lesson 7. Signalling. 1 Samuel 20:20–22; 35–39.

Lesson 8. Lay and Light a Fire. Fire Lighting Contest. 1 Kings 18: 22–24.

First class scout

Lesson 8. Signalling. Daniel 5: 1–31.

Lesson 9. Go on Foot to a Given Point and Return and Give a Report of the Trip. Numbers 13:1–3; 17–21; 23–33.

Lesson 10. Produce an Article of Carpentry, Joinery or Metal Work. 2 Chronicles 2:11–16.

Lesson 11. Bring a Tenderfoot Trained in the Points Required for a Tenderfoot. John 1: 40–42.

The scout law

Lesson 12. A Scout's Honour is to be Trusted. Genesis 39:7–10.

Lesson 13. Loyalty. Esther 4:8–16.

Lesson 14. A Scout is a Friend to All, and Must NEVER BE A SNOB. Luke 9:46–48.

Lesson 15. A Friend to Animals. 1 Samuel 17:12–16.

Lesson 16. Obey Orders. Jonah 1:1–3.

Lesson 17. Cheerfulness and Willingness. Acts 16 :25; Philippians 4:11–13.

Lesson 18. Thrift. Matthew 6:19–21.

The great scout master

Lesson 19. Matthew 23:10.

Novel Bonfire

The author experienced something very unusual one Sunday afternoon in a camp where he was invited to speak. The talk was on 'Trees or Growth,' one of the studies of the course described. During the talk a number of things were referred to that enter into the growth of a tree which either mar or hinder it from becoming a symmetrical, beautiful tree and a similar comparison was made regarding a boy's growth. The question was asked of the boys, 'What are some of the things which interfere with a boy's growth physically, mentally and morally?' A number of things, such as smoking, swearing, impurity, etc., were given, and finally one of the small boys piped up 'reading dime novels.' His answer was received with howls of derision, especially from the older boys. 'Hold on,' I said, 'let's discuss the matter; if dime novels are good for a boy's growth mentally, we want to know about it, but if they are detrimental to this particular kind of desired growth, of course, we want to cut it out.' The discussion brought out the fact that a number of the boys had smuggled a lot of this kind of literature into camp and were just loafing through their time in the woods, gloating over the wonderful and daring escapades of Wild West heroes. The boys finally decided that their mental growth was retarded by such reading. Then came the question, 'What are you going to do about it?' 'We don't usually have a bonfire on Sunday,' I said. "I am inclined, however, to ask your leader for a special dispensation and we will have one. You are to furnish the fuel, your leader the kerosene oil and I will provide the match. The fuel is to consist of all the dime novels in the camp.' 'Whew!' 'I know it will take grit to do this, but it is a test of your sincerity and determination to progress along right lines.' 'We're game?' yelled the boys, 'and we mean business.'

The start was made for the place where the bonfires were usually held. By the time I reached the spot, the boys were coming from their tents with bundles of novels. Every boy was requested to tear each novel in half and throw it upon the heap. When everything was ready, the boys uncovered and in the silence that came upon the group, the match was struck and the flames began to leap upward, until finally, all that remained was the small piles of ashes. For the majority of the boys it meant the burning up of the dross and the beginning of better and nobler thinking. I shall always remember this novel bonfire. This is what I mean by making Bible study and camp talks effective.

Reading

Sunday afternoon is the time for reading good, wholesome stories. Take the boys out into the woods where they can squat under a big tree, or if the day is warm seek the cool shelter of the tent and while the boys are lying down read a short story or several chapters of a story like *Dr. Grenfell's Parish*, by Norman Duncan, *Just Boys*, by Mary Buell Wood, *Some Boys I Know*, *Chapel Talks*, or *The Story of Good Will Farm*, by George W. Hinckley. If the group is made up of older boys who like to discuss life problems, read a chapter or two from Robert Speer's excellent books, *A Young Man's Questions* and *Young Men Who Overcame*. Make sure that whatever you read has the uplift note. The real purpose of the afternoon's reading should be that of instilling in the boys' minds some of the cardinal virtues of Christian character.

Don't moralise; let the story do its own moralising. Boys are hero worshippers. If the hero or the heroic appeal of the story is of a sane type and not abnormal there will be created naturally within the boy a desire to emulate the good deeds of the hero in the everyday life of the camp, which is much better than the parrot-like vocalisation unfortunately many times encouraged by well-meaning men.

Chapel

A pile of stones made to serve as an altar or pulpit, a chapel having the branches of a friendly pine as its roof and under which are built a reading desk and seats of white birch, a cathedral with towering columns of pine and cushions of pine needles, a rocky shore along the ocean – all are places where boys have heard the appeal for right living and responded with an earnest decision that marked an advance step in their moral and religious growth.

Make much of the music at these outdoor services on Sunday. A choir of men and boys responding in the distance to the hymns of the camp boys, in antiphonal manner, a cornetist playing a hymn in the distance, make an impression never to be forgotten.

The great test of camp life is not the fun the boy had, or his gain in weight, height or lung capacity, or the friendships formed, or his increased knowledge in woodcraft, but his advancement in character-making and gain in spiritual vigour.

Bibliography

Books helpful in the preparation of Bible study:
Lessons from Life (Animal and Human) – Thomas Whittaker. Macmillan.
Sermons in Stones – Amos R. Wells. Doubleday, Page & Company.
Parables from Nature – Mrs Gatty. Colportage Library.
A Good Bible Dictionary and Concordance.

Books upon the religious life of boys:
The Boy and the Church – Eugene C. Foster. The Sunday School Times Co.
Starting to Teach Eugene – C. Foster. Association Press.
The Child and His Religion – George E. Dawson. University of Chicago.
Religion in Boyhood – Ernest B. Layard. E.P. Dutton and Company.

9

Food – Its Function, Purchase, Preparation, Cooking, Serving

We may live without friends, we may live without books, but civilised man cannot live without cooks.

Good Cooking

The normal boy sums up life in two words of three letters each: 'F-u-n' and 'E-a-t.' As long as there is plenty of fun and plenty to eat, he thinks life is worth living, and he is not so far from the truth, for it is only when the fun of living dies within us, and our digestive apparatus refuses to do its function that we 'become of all men most miserable.' A boy will put up with all sorts of inconvenience but rebels at once at poor food and bad cooking. The good nature, congenial atmosphere, and contentedness of camp life is largely due to good cooking. Economise in every other way, but think twice before cheap cooks are employed or a cheap grade of food purchased.

A good cook will economise, he knows what to do with leftovers and how to prepare menus of variety. The quantity of swill soon reveals the worth of the cook. In a large camp £100 may easily find its way into the litter bin because of cheap cooks and poor food. A growing boy demands relatively more of the tissue-building kind of food than a grown person, because the body is being built up. When the full stature is reached the tissue-building part of the food is only required to take the place of that worn out each day. Professor Atwater has told us that the boy of fifteen or sixteen requires ninety per cent of the food ration of the adult man engaged in moderate muscular work. Boys at twelve require seventy per cent.

Vegetables, fruits, cereals, bread, nuts and meats furnish the essentials. Sugar and fat have only part of them. Coffee and tea have no food values except for the milk and sugar added. They tend to check certain normal secretion in the body and should not be used during growth.

Food Charts

Leaders and cooks will find the following food charts of exceptional value in providing and planning the food for the boys. Boys will be interested in the information given and the attractive form of presentation. The following table is a condensation of the facts given on the charts, and will help in planning menus:

Prepared by C.F. LANGWORTHY.
Expert in charge of Nutrition Investigation.

Chart 1	Protein	Fat	Carbohydrates	Ash	Water	Calories per
Whole milk	3.3	4.0	5.0	0.7	87.0	310
Skim milk	3.4	0.3	5.1	0.7	90.5	165
Buttermilk	3.0	0.5	4.8	0.7	91.0	160
Cream	2.5	18.5	4.5	2.5	74.0	865

Chart 2	Protein	Fat	Carbohydrates	Ash	Water	Calories per
Whole egg	14.8	10.5	–	1.0	73.7	700
Egg white	13.0	0.2	–	0.6	86.2	265
Egg yolk	16.1	33.3	–	1.1	49.5	1608
Cream cheese	25.9	33.7	2.4	3.8	34.2	1950
Cottage cheese	20.9	1.0	4.3	1.8	72.0	510

Chart 3 (edible portion of)	Protein	Fat	Carbohydrates	Ash	Water	Calories per
Lamb chop	17.6	28.3	–	1.0	53.1	1540
Pork	16.9	30.1	–	1.0	52.0	1580
Smoked ham	16.1	38.8	–	4.8	40.3	1940
Beefsteak	18.6	18.5	–	1.0	61.9	1130
Dried beef	30.0	6.6	–	9.1	54.3	840

Chart 4	Protein	Fat	Carbohydrates	Ash	Water	Calories per
Cod, lean fish	15.8	0.4	–	1.2	82.6	325
Cod, Salt	21.5	0.3	–	24.7	53.5	410
Oyster	6.2	1.2	3.7	2.0	86.9	235
Smoked herring	36.4	15.8	–	13.2	34.6	1355
Mackerel, fat	18.3	7.1	–	1.2	73.4	645

Chart 5	Protein	Fat	Carbohydrates	Ash	Water	Calories per
Olive Oil	–	100.0	–	–	–	4080
Bacon	9.4	67.4	–	4.4	18.8	3030
Beef suet	4.7	81.8	–	0.3	13.2	3510
Butter	1.0	85.0	–	3.0	11.0	3410
Lard	–	100.0	–	–	–	4080

Chart 6	Protein	Fat	Carbohydrates	Ash	Water	Calories per
Corn	10.0	4.3	73.4	1.5	10.8	1800
Wheat	12.2	1.7	73.7	1.8	10.6	1750
Buckwheat	10.0	2.2	73.2	2.0	12.6	1600
Oat	11.8	5.0	69.2	3.0	11.0	1720
Rice	8.0	2.0	77.0	1.0	12.0	1720
Rye	12.2	1.5	73.9	1.9	10.5	1750

Chart 7	Protein	Fat	Carbohydrates	Ash	Water	Calories per
White bread	9.2	1.3	53.1	1.1	35.3	1215
Whole wheat bread	9.7	0.9	49.7	1.3	38.4	1140
Oat breakfast food (cooked)	2.8	0.5	11.5	0.7	84.5	285
Toasted bread	11.5	1.6	61.2	1.7	24.0	1420
Cornbread	7.9	4.7	46.3	2.2	38.9	1205
Macaroni	3.0	1.5	15.8	1.3	78.4	415

Chart 8	Protein	Fat	Carbohydrates	Ash	Water	Calories per
Sugar, granulated	–	100.0	–	–	–	1860
Molasses	2.4	–	69.3	3.2	25.1	1290
Stick candy	–	–	96.5	0.5	3.0	1785
Maple sugar	–	–	82.8	0.9	16.3	1540
Honey	0.4	–	81.2	0.2	18.2	1520

Chart 9	Protein	Fat	Carbohydrates	Ash	Water	Calories per
Parsnip	1.6	0.5	13.5	1.4	83.0	230
Onion	1.6	0.3	9.9	0.6	87.6	225
Potato	2.2	0.1	18.4	1.0	78.3	385
Celery	1.1	–	3.4	1.0	94.5	8

Chart 10	Protein	Fat	Carbohydrates	Ash	Water	Calories per
Shelled beans, fresh	9.4	0.6	29.1	2.0	58.9	740
Navy beans, dry	22.5	1.8	59.6	3.5	12.6	1600
String beans, green	2.3	0.3	7.4	0.8	89.2	195
Corn, green	3.1	1.1	19.7	0.7	75.4	500

Chart 11	Protein	Fat	Carbohydrates	Ash	Water	Calories per
Apple (edible portion)	0.4	0.5	14.2	0.3	84.6	290
Fried fig	4.3	0.3	74.2	2.4	18.8	1475
Strawberry	1.0	0.6	7.4	0.6	90.4	180
Banana	1.3	0.6	22.0	0.8	75.3	460

Chart 12	Protein	Fat	Carbohydrates	Ash	Water	Calories per
Grapes (edible portion)	1.3	1.6	19.2	0.5	77.4	450
Raisins	2.6	3.3	76.1	3.4	14.6	1605
Canned fruit	1.1	0.1	21.1	0.5	77.2	415
Fruit jelly	–	–	78.3	0.7	21.0	1455
Grape juice	0.2	–	7.4	0.2	92.2	150

Chart 13	Protein	Fat	Carbohydrates	Ash	Water	Calories per
Walnut	16.6	63.4	16.1	1.4	2.5	3285
Chestnut	10.7	7.0	74.2	2.2	5.9	1875
Peanut	25.8	38.6	22.4	2.0	9.2	2500
Peanut butter	29.3	46.5	17.1	5.0	2.1	2825
Coconut, desiccated	6.3	57.4	31.5	1.3	3.5	3121

Chart 14 Functions and Uses of Food; Constituent of Food

Food as purchased contains:

Edible Portion   Flesh of meat, yolk and white of eggs, wheat flour, etc
                  Protein
                  Fats
                  Carbohydrates
                  Mineral matter or ash

Refuse   Bones, entrails, shells, bran, etc.

Use of Food in the Body:
        Protein builds and repairs tissue
        White (albumen) of eggs
        Curd of milk
        Lean meat, gluten of wheat, etc
        Carbohydrates are transferred into fat, sugar, starch, etc.
All serve as fuel to yield energy in the forms of heat and muscular power
        Mineral Matter or Ash share in forming bone, assist in digestion, etc.
        Phosphate of lime.
        Potash, soda, etc.
Food is that which, taken into the body, builds tissue or yields energy.

Chart 15 Dietary standard for man in full vigour at moderate muscular work

Condition Considered	Protein Grams	Energy Calories
Food as purchased	115	3,800
Food eaten	100	3,500
Food digested	95	3,200

Estimated amount of mineral matter required per man per day:

	Grams
Phosphoric acid (P_2O_5)	3 to 4
Calcium oxide	0.7 to 1.0
Sulphuric acid (SO_3)	2 to 3.5
Magnesium oxide	0.3 to 0.5
Potassium oxide	2 to 3
Iron	0.006 to 0.012
Sodium oxide	4 to 6
Chlorine	6 to 8

Time required for Digestion of various Foods:

	Hrs	Min
Apples, sweet	1	30
Apples, sour	2	
Beans, pod, boiled	2	30
Beef, fresh, rare roasted	3	
Beef, dried	3	30
Beets, boiled	3	45
Bread, wheat, fresh	3	40
Bread corn	3	15
Butter (melted)	3	30
Cabbage, raw, with vinegar	2	
Cabbage, boiled	4	30
Cheese	3	30
Codfish	2	
Custard, baked	2	45
Ducks, wild, roasted	4	30
Eggs, fresh, soft boiled	3	
Eggs, fresh, hard boiled	3	30
Eggs, fresh, fried	3	30
Lamb, fresh, boiled	2	30
Milk, raw	2	15
Milk, boiled	2	
Parsnips, boiled	2	30
Mutton, roast	3	15
Mutton, boiled	3	
Mutton, broiled	3	
Pork, roast	5	15
Potato, boiled	3	30
Potato, baked	2	30
Rice, boiled	1	

Sago, boiled	1	45
Salmon, boiled	4	
Soup, beef, vegetable	4	
Soup, chicken	3	
Tapioca, boiled	2	
Trout, boiled or fried	1	30
Turnips, boiled	3	30
Veal, fresh, boiled	4	

Food naturally falls into four classes: Potatoes and grains furnish starches. The starchy foods are heat and force producers. Eggs, meats, nuts, milk, dried beans, peas and lentils furnish nitrogen, and are flesh and muscle producers. Butter, oil, lard, and fatty meats supply fats. Sugar, molasses, honey, fruit, etc., furnish sugar.

Starchy foods should be cooked at a high temperature and either boiled or baked; nitrogenous and fatty foods at lower temperature, prolonging the time. Meats are much better broiled, roasted, or stewed than fried. Vegetables should be steamed or baked so that the juices may not be wasted. Veal and pork (except ham and bacon) should have no place in the menu of a boys' summer camp. Both require from four to five hours and fifteen minutes to digest. Study carefully the above tables and then plan your meals intelligently.

Table of Approximate Weights and Measures

Three teaspoonfuls = one tablespoon.
Four tablespoonfuls = one wine glass.
Two wine glasses = one gill.
Two gills = one tumbler or cup.
Two cupfuls = one pint.
One quart sifted flour = one pound.
One quart granulated sugar = one pound, nine ounces.
One pint closely packed butter = one pound.
Three cupfuls sugar = one pound.
Five cupfuls sifted flour = one pound.
One tablespoonful salt = one ounce.
Seven tablespoonfuls granulated sugar = one half pint.
Twelve tablespoonfuls flour = one pint.
Three coffee cupfuls = one quart.
Ten eggs = one pound.

Buying Food

The purchase of food is an important item of expense in operating a boys' camp, large or small. If the camp is a large one, 100 or more boys, and you have a good-sized refrigerator and storehouse, always purchase in bulk form from a wholesale firm. Canned goods, such as peas, tomatoes, corn, and apples, buy in gallon cans in case lots and save cost of extra tin and labels. Cocoa may be purchased in five-pound cans. Condensed milk (unsweetened) in 20-ounce cans. Flour and sugar by the barrel. Beans by the bushel. Butter by the firkin.[1] For instance, a good heavy 200-pound hind quarter of beef will furnish a roast beef dinner, a steak breakfast, a meat stew supper, a meat hash breakfast, and a good thick soup full of nourishment from the bones. The suet may be rendered into lard. There will be no waste, and you get the very best of meat. Buy lamb whole and fowl cleaned, and eggs by the crate. Keep an accurate inventory, also the cost of foods. It will be found interesting to make a resume of food at the end of each season, listing quantities, costs, and amounts used each day and ascertain the actual cost per day for each boy.

The following 'Grocery List' is for a large camp, but it will serve also to form the basis of providing for small camps:

Cocoa	Raisins (seeded)
Coffee	Currants
Sugar (granulated)	Flour
Beans, yellow	Graham flour
Beans, red kidney	Corn starch
Tapioca	Gelatine
Rice	Figs
Oatmeal (in bulk)	Prunes
Cornmeal	Evaporated fruits
Toasted Corn Flakes	Codfish cakes
Cream of Wheat	Macaroni
Shredded Wheat	Crackers
Salt (table)	Ginger Snaps
Salt (rock)	Pilot Biscuits
Pepper, black	Extracts:
Ginger	Vanilla, Lemon
Cloves	Kitchen Boquet (for gravy)
Soda	Chocolate cake
Cinnamon	Lemons
Baking Powder	Olive Oil
Cream of Tartar	Vinegar
Magic yeast	Lard

Butter	Chilli Sauce
Eggs	Bacon
Onions	Ham
Potatoes	Dried beef
Sapolio (soap)	Salt pork
Gold Dust	Cheese
Laundry soap	Matches
Mustard (dry)	Candles
Mustard (prepared in mugs)	Kerosene oil
Chow Chow	Lantern wicks
Pickles	Chloride of Lime.
Piccalilli	

Canned goods:

Corn; sliced peaches; tomatoes; shredded pineapple; peas; strawberries; lima beans; clams (for chowder); beets; condensed milk (unsweetened); apples; salmon; plums.

The Steward

A reliable person should be in charge of the food supplies. In some camps he is called the Steward. He will see that the supply is sufficient, arrange the menus in consultation with the chef, keep his storeroom neat and scrupulously clean. As a matter of record and for the purpose of ascertaining cost of feeding the boys, a number of camps keep a daily record like the illustrated form.

The Cook

The cook is the keynote of happiness or unhappiness. Get a good cook, professionally and morally, one who understands that he is not in camp for a vacation. A capable cook will take care of fifty boys without any assistance, except what help the boys may render in the preparation of vegetables. For years two cooks have looked after the meals of 175 to 200 boys in the camps conducted each season by the writer. Some camps secure cooks from the hotels and restaurants, others from the lumber camps. No matter where he is secured, be sure that he is clean, in person, in habits, and in speech. Do not permit boys to loaf about the kitchen. In the planning of menus, food value and variety must be considered. The following represents the staple articles of food for a boys' camp.

Commissary Department, Camp Becket

Suggested List of Dishes for Boys' Camps

Breakfast

Fruit: Bananas, raspberries, blueberries, cantaloupes, apples, stewed prunes, applesauce, baked apples, stewed apples, stewed apricots, stewed figs.

Cereals: Oatmeal, Shredded Wheat, Cream of Wheat, Toasted Corn Flakes; corn meal mush and milk, Hominy Grits, Puffed Rice, Wheatlets.

Eggs: Fried, boiled, scrambled, omelette, poached on toast.

Meats and Fish: Bacon, meat hash, meat stew, chopped meat on toast, codfish cakes, creamed codfish, fried fresh fish, creamed dried beef, fresh sausage.

Vegetables: Potatoes – Baked, creamed, mashed, browned, German fried; baked beans.

Drinks: Cocoa, milk, coffee (only occasionally), pure water.

Bread: Toasted bread, corn bread, muffins, biscuits, hot cakes.

Dinner

Soups: Old-fashioned vegetable soup, bean soup, clam or fish chowder, corn chowder. Thick soups are preferable for camps.

Meats: Roasts – beef, lamb, chicken. Stews – beef, lamb, steak, fricassee of chicken, fricassee of lamb, haricot of lamb, pot roast of beef, Hamburg steak, corned beef, boiled ham, meat pie.

Fish: Baked, fried, boiled; escalloped salmon, salmon croquettes.

Vegetables: Potatoes – mashed, boiled, French fried, browned. Cabbage. Corn – stewed, escalloped, corn pie, corn on cob. Peas – creamed with carrots. Lima beans. Summer squash. Tomatoes – stewed, escalloped, au gratin with tomatoes. Apple sauce, creamed onions; cabbage slaw. Greens-spinach, beet tops.

Desserts: Ice-Cream – vanilla, chocolate, strawberry (preserved), raspberry, lemon, coffee, caramel, peach, pineapple (shredded), orange, lemon. Sherbet – lemon, orange, pineapple, raspberry. Rice pudding, plain with fruit sauce, rice with raisins. Tapioca pudding with apples or fruit. Bread pudding. Cottage pudding, lemon sauce or fruit sauce. Banana pudding. Sliced peaches with cream. Pie – apple, blueberry, blackberry. Cornstarch pudding.

Supper

Cereals: Cream of Wheat, mush and milk, Shredded Wheat.

Cold Dishes: Sliced beef, ham, corned beef, potato salad, cabbage slaw, pressed meats.

Hot Dishes: Irish stew, meat croquettes, frankfurters, potato cakes, baked beans, thick soups, stewed kidney beans. Potatoes – baked, fried, creamed. Creamed salmon with peas; codfish; macaroni and cheese; potato hash.

Desserts: Prunes, stewed apples, stewed apricots, fresh fruits, stewed pears, stewed figs.

Cakes: Gingerbread, sweetbread, cookies.

Relishes: Pickles beets, chow chow, piccalilli, watermelon spiced.

Drinks: Lemonade, iced tea, cocoa, hot milk.

Local geographical conditions will suggest a variety of dishes. There should be plenty of milk to drink, and good bread and butter. Cake and fancy dishes are not necessary. The bill of fare should be an elastic one. When the day is cold and dreary, hot chowders, soups, cocoa, etc., should be served.

On a warm day, lemonade and cold dishes are desirable. Every camp should, if possible, have its own ice-cream freezer, as ice-creams, sherbets, and water ices are not only healthy but inexpensive. An occasional delicacy is desirable. Canned shredded pineapple, strawberries and sliced peaches make excellent sherbets and ice cream. In one camp chicken and ice cream are served every Sunday dinner.

A Sample Week of Menus

Breakfast	Dinner	Supper
Monday		
Oatmeal Fried potatoes Cocoa Cream of tartar biscuits	Irish stew Boiled potatoes Green corn on the cob Apple tapioca Bread and butter	Fried eggs Prunes Sweet cake Bread and butter Cocoa
Tuesday		
Toasted cornflakes Fish cakes Corn bread Cocoa	Beef steak Mashed potatoes Peas Corn starch pudding Bread and butter	Vegetable soup Stewed figs Gingerbread Bread and butter
Wednesday		
Cream of wheat Meat hash Cocoa Bread and butter	Roast lamb Tomato sauce Boiled potatoes Lemon sherbet Bread and butter	Creamed fish Apple sauce Sweet cake Bread and butter
Thursday		
Shredded wheat Baked potatoes Creamed codfish Bread and butter Cocoa	Boiled beef Mashed potatoes Corn starch pudding with strawberry sauce	Creamed dried beef Apple sauce Gingerbread Bread and butter
Friday		
Oatmeal Codfish cakes Bread and butter Cocoa	Fried weak fish Stewed tomatoes Boiled potatoes Vanilla ice cream	Vegetable soup Bread and butter Sweet cake
Saturday		
Puffed rice Fried eggs Bread and butter Cocoa	Escalloped salmon Rice Boiled tomatoes Cucumbers Bread and butter	Boston baked beans Tomato catsup Sweetbread
Sunday		
Cream of wheat Bananas Fried mush and maple syrup Coffee	Roast chicken Creamed onions Mashed potatoes Pineapple sherbet Bread and butter	Cold beef Apple sauce Sweet cake Bread and butter

Serving

Each table is provided with a meat platter, vegetable dishes, bread plate, butter dish, sugar bowl, milk pitcher, water pitcher, salt and pepper shakers, etc. The only need of a waiter is to bring the food to the tables and replenish the dishes. Each boy takes his turn at waiting. If there are seven boys in a tent, a boy serves one day in seven. He usually sits at the right side of the leader and eats his meal with the others. This does away with a second or 'waiter' table. By this system you avoid the tendency to smartness and roughness. Each leader is careful to see that food is not wasted at his table, that decency and order is preserved, and wholesome conversation and pleasantries indulged in during the meal, as an aid to good digestion.

Dishwashing

Some camps pay for all work done and give boys more freedom, but experience has clearly proven that the successful camp is the one where boys all have responsibility and definite duties to perform. Dishwashing is never attractive. It may be made less irksome by carefully systematising the work. There are several ways. One way is that of having each boy wash his own dishes, working a tent at a time. A number of tubs of hot, soapy water are provided for washing, and several extra tubs filled with very hot water for rinsing. At a signal from the camp director or person in charge, each table of boys by rotation passes from the dining room with the dishes to these tubs and each boy proceeds to do his own dishwashing and rinsing and drying. Another way is to provide two good-sized dish-pans for each table, and assign two boys to do the dish-washing for the day. The dishes are washed at the tables and stowed away in a closet, each table having its own closet. Another way is to purchase a good dish-washing machine, and install it in the kitchen.

Cleanliness must be insisted upon. Never leave anything unwashed until it is used again. The eating from dirty and greasy plates, forks, knives, and spoons will result in disease. No matter what system you use, do not let down on dirty dishes.

A Few Hints

Soup
'Soup makes the soldier,' said Napoleon I. Bones should never be thrown away, but cracked and placed in stock pot, covered with water and let simmer. This makes 'stock' which is the foundation of all soup.

All green vegetables should be washed well in cold water and put in boiling salted water, and boiled slowly until tender. All white and underground vegetables should be cooked in boiling unsalted water, the salt being added at the last moment.

Potatoes take from twenty to thirty minutes to boil. In boiling and roasting allow about a quarter of an hour for every pound of meat. The fire should be medium hot. Boiled fish should be cooked ten minutes to each pound.

Water

Water is the only true beverage. Forming as it does three-quarters of the weight of the human body, it is of next importance to the air we breathe. Milk is a food and not a beverage.

Onions

Peel or slice onions in water and you will not shed tears.

Egg Test

To test the freshness of an egg, drop into cold water. If the egg sinks quickly it is fresh, if it stands on end it is doubtful, and quite bad if it floats. The shell of a fresh egg looks dull; a stale one is glossy.

Mending Pots

A pot may be mended by making a paste of flour, salt and fine wood ashes. Plaster it on where the leak is and let it dry before using.

Table Etiquette

A mother complained that her boy, after being in camp for two weeks, returned home speaking a new language, particularly at the dining table. If he wanted milk, he called for 'cow', butter was 'goat', biscuits were 'sinkers', meat was 'corpse', and there were several other terms and phrases peculiar to camp life. He had to learn all over the ways of decency and reasonable table refinement. There is no plausible reason why this should be so in a boys' camp. Grabbing of food, yelling for food, upsetting of liquids, and table 'rough-house' will be largely prevented by the system of seating and of serving. The most satisfactory way is to seat by tent groups. Have as many tables as you have tents. Let each tent leader preside at the head of his table, and serve the food in family style. The leader serves the food, and sees that the boys observe the same delightful table life in camp as at home.

Grace at Meals

Grace should be said before each meal, either silently or audibly. In the morning the hymn on the following page is sung by the boys at one camp, followed with bowed heads in silent prayer:

Music for morning prayer hymn for boy's camp

Morning Prayer Hymn for Boys' Camps

To be sung at morning meal
Words and Music by H.W. Gibbon.

Morning

   Gracious Giver of all good,
     Thee we thank for rest and food.
   Grant that all we do or say
     In Thy service be this day.

Noon

   Father for this noonday meal
     We would speak the praise we feel,
   Health and strength we have from Thee,
     Help us, Lord, to faithful be.

Night

   Tireless guardian of our way,
     Thou hast kept us well this day.
   While we thank Thee, we request
     Care continued, pardon, rest.

   Go abroad upon the paths of Nature,
   And when all its voices whisper, and its silent things
   Are breathing the deep beauty of the world –
   Kneel at its ample altar.

                              (Bryant)

10

The Camp Fire

There is an impalpable, invisible, softly stepping delight in the camp fire which escapes analysis. Enumerate all its charms, and still there is something missing in your catalogue.

(W.C. Gray in *Camp Fire Musings*)

I cannot conceive of a camp that does not have a big fire! Our city houses do not have it, not even a fireplace. The fireplace is one of the greatest schools the imagination has ever had or ever can have. It is moral, and it always gives a tremendous stimulus to the imagination, and that is why stories and fire go together. You cannot tell a good story unless you tell it before a fire. You cannot have a complete fire unless you have a good story-teller along.[1]

Anyone who has witnessed a real camp fire and participated in its fun, as well as seriousness, will never forget it. The huge fire shooting up its tongue of flame into the darkness of the night, the perfect shower of golden rain, the company of happy boys, and great, dark background of piney woods, the weird light over all, the singing, the yells, the stories, the fun, then the serious word at the close, is a happy experience long to be remembered.

To Build a Fire

There are ways and ways of building camp fires. An old Indian saying runs, 'White man heap fool, make um big fire – can't git near! Injun make um little fire – git close! Uh! good!' Make it a service privilege for a tent of boys to gather wood and build the fire. This should be done during the afternoon. Two things are essential in the building of a fire – kindling and air. A fire must be built systematically. First, get dry, small dead branches, twigs, fir branches and other inflammable material. Place these upon the ground. Be sure that air can draw under the pile and up through it. Next place some heavier branches in tripod form over the kindling, then good-sized sticks, and so on until you have built the camp fire the required size. In many camps it is considered an honour to light the fire.

Kerosene oil may be poured upon the kindling, or old newspapers used in lighting the fire.

Caution

Be sure to use every precaution to prevent the spreading of fire. This may be done by building a circle of stone around the fire, or by digging up the earth, or by wetting a space around the fire. Always have buckets of water near at hand.

Things to remember:
First, It is criminal to leave a burning fire;
Second, Always put out the fire with water or earth.

To Light a Match

Kephart, in his book on *Camping and Woodcraft* (page 88), says,

When there is nothing dry to strike it on, jerk the head of the match forward through the teeth. Face the wind. Cup your hands, backs toward wind. Remove right hand just long enough to strike match on something very close by, then instantly resume former position. Flame of match will run up the stick instead of blowing away from it.

Story-Telling

The camp fire is a golden opportunity for the telling of stories – good stories told well. Indian legends, war stories, ghost stories, detective stories, stories of heroism, the history of fire, a talk about the stars. Don't drag out the telling of a story. Talk it in boy language. Avoid technical terms. Make the story live.

College songs always appeal to boys. Let some leader start up a song in a natural way, and soon you will have a chorus of unexpected melody and harmony. As the fire dies down, let the songs be of a more quiet type.

Roast Delight

When the embers are glowing is the time for toasting marshmallows. Get a long stick sharpened to a point, fasten a marshmallow on the end, hold it over the embers, not in the blaze, until the marshmallow expands. Oh, the deliciousness of it! Ever tasted one? Before roasting corn on the cob, tie the end of each husk firmly with string. Soak in water for about an hour. Then put into the hot embers. The water prevents the corn from burning and the firmly tied husks enable the corn to be steamed and the real corn flavour is retained. In about twenty minutes the corn may be taken from the fire and eaten. Have a bowl of melted butter and salt on hand. Also a pastry brush to spread the melted butter upon the corn. Try it.

A Good Story

For an example of a good story to be told around the camp fire, this Indian tale by Professor H.M. Burr, of the Springfield Training School, is given:

How men found the great spirit

In the olden time, when woods covered all the earth except the deserts and the river bottoms, and men lived on the fruits and berries they found and the wild animals which they could shoot or snare; when they dressed in skins and lived in caves, there was little time for thought. But as men grew stronger and more cunning and learned how to live together, they had more time to think and more mind to think with.

Men had learned many things. They had learned that cold weather followed hot, and spring followed winter, and that the sun got up in the morning and went to bed at night. They saw that the great water was kindly when the sun shone, but when the sun hid its face and the wind blew upon it, it grew black and angry and upset their canoes. They found that knocking flints together or rubbing dry sticks would light the dry moss and that the flames, which would bring back summer in the midst of winter and day in the midst of night, were hungry and must be fed, and when they escaped devoured the woods and only the water could stop them.

These and many other things men learned, but no one knew why it all was or how it came to be. Men began to wonder – and that was the beginning of the path which led to the Great Spirit.

In the ages when men began to wonder there was born a boy whose name was 'Wo,' which meant in the language of his time 'Whence.' As he lay in his mother's arms, she loved him and wondered, 'His body is of my body, but from whence comes the life – the spirit which is like mine and yet not like it?' And his father, seeing the wonder in the mother's eyes, said: 'Whence came he from?' And there was no one to answer, and so they called him 'Wo,' to remind them that they knew not from whence he came.

As Wo grew up, he was stronger and swifter of foot than any of his tribe. He became a mighty hunter. He knew the ways of all the wild things, and could read the signs of the season. As he grew older they made him a chief and listened while he spoke at the council board, but Wo was not satisfied. His name was a question, and questioning filled his mind.

From whence did he come? Whither was he going? Why did the sun rise and set? Why did life burst into leaf and flower with the coming of the spring? Why did the child become a man and the man grow old and die?

The mystery grew upon him as he pondered. In the morning he stood on a mountain top and, stretching out his hands, cried: 'Whence?' At night he cried to the moon: 'Whither?' He listened to the soughing of the trees and the song of the brook and tried to learn their language. He peered eagerly into the eyes of little children, and tried to read the mystery of life. He listened at the still lips of the dead, waiting for them to tell him whither they had gone.

He went about among his fellows silent and absorbed, always looking for the unseen and listening for the unspoken. He sat so long silent at the council board that the elders questioned him. To their questioning he replied, like one awakening from a dream:

'Our fathers since the beginning have trailed the beasts of the woods. There is none so cunning as the fox, but we can trail him to his lair. Though we are weaker than the great bear and buffalo, yet by our wisdom we overcome them. The deer is more swift of foot, but by craft we overtake him. We cannot fly like a bird, but we snare the winged one with a hair. We have made ourselves many cunning inventions by which the beasts, the trees, the wind, the water, and the fire become our servants.

Then we speak great swelling words: How great and wise we are! There is none like us in the air, in the wood, or in the water!

'But the words are false. Our pride is like that of a partridge drumming on his log in the wood before the fox leaps upon him. Our sight is like that of the mole burrowing under the ground. Our wisdom is like a drop of dew upon the grass. Our ignorance is like the great water which no eye can measure.

'Our life is like a bird coming out of the dark, fluttering for a heart-beat in the tepee and then going forth into the dark again. No one can tell us whence it comes or whither it goes. I have asked the wise men, and they cannot answer; I have listened to the voice of the trees and wind and water, but I do not know their tongue; I have questioned the sun and the moon and the stars, but they are silent.

'But to-day, in the silence before the darkness gives place to light, I seemed to hear a still small voice within my breast, saying to me: "Wo, the questioner, rise up like the stag from his lair; away, alone, to the mountain of the sun. There thou shalt find that which thou seekest."

'I go, but if I fall by the trail another will take it up. If I find the answer I will return.'

Waiting for none, Wo left the council of his tribe and went his way toward the mountain of the sun. For six days he made his way through the trackless woods, guided by the sun by day and the stars by night. On the seventh he came to the great mountain – the mountain of the sun – on whose top, according to the tradition of his tribe, the sun rested each night. All day long he climbed, saying to himself: 'I will sleep to-night in the tepee of the sun and he will tell me whence I come and whither I go.'

But as he climbed the sun seemed to climb higher and higher. As he neared the top a cold cloud settled like a night bird on the mountain. Chilled and faint with hunger and fatigue, Wo struggled on. Just at sunset he reached the top of the mountain, but it was not the mountain of the sun, for many days' journey to the west the sun was sinking in the Great Water.

A bitter cry broke from Wo's parched lips. His long trail was useless. There was no answer to his questions. The sun journeyed farther and faster than men dreamed, and of wood and waste and water there was no end. Overcome with misery and weakness, he fell upon a bed of moss with his back toward the sunset and the unknown.

And Wo slept, although it was unlike any sleep he had ever known before, and as he slept he dreamed. He was alone upon the mountain waiting for the answer. A cloud covered the mountain, but all was silent. A mighty wind rent the cloud and rushed roaring through the crags, but there was no voice in the wind. Thunder pealed, lightning flashed, but he whom Wo sought was not there.

In the hush that followed the storm Wo heard a voice low and quiet, but in it all the sounds of earth and sky seemed to mingle – the song of the bird, the whispering of the trees, and the murmuring of the brook.

'Wo, I am He whom thou seekest; I am the Great Spirit; I am the All-Father. Ever since I made man of the dust of the earth and so child of the earth and brother to all living, and breathed into his nostrils the breath of life, thus making him My son, I have waited for a seeker who should find Me. In the fullness of time thou hast come, Wo, the questioner, to the Answerer.

'Thy body is of the earth and to earth returns; thy spirit is Mine; it is given thee for a space to make according to thy will; then it returns to Me better or worse for thy making.

'Thou hast found Me because thy heart was pure and thy search for Me tireless. Go back to thy tribe and be to them the voice of the Great Spirit. From henceforth I will speak to thee and the seekers that come after thee, in a thousand voices and appear in a thousand shapes. I will speak in the voices of the wood and streams and of those you love. I will appear to you in the sun by day and the stars by night. When thy people and Mine are in need and wish for the will of the Great Spirit, then shall My spirit brood over thine and the words that thou shalt speak shall be My words.'

And Wo awoke, facing the east and the rising sun. His body was warmed by its rays. A great gladness filled his soul. He had sought and found, and prayer came to him like the song to the bird:

'O Great Spirit, Father of my spirit, the sun is Thy messenger, but Thou art brighter than the sun. Drive Thou the darkness before me. Be Thou the light of my spirit.'

As Wo went down the mountain and took the journey back to the home of his people his face shone, and the light never seemed to leave it, so that men called him 'He of the shining face.'

When Wo came back to his tribe, all who saw his face knew that he had found the answer, and they gathered again about the council fire to hear. As Wo stood up and looked into the eager faces in the circle of the fire, he remembered that the Great Spirit had given him no message, and for a moment he was dumb. Then the words of the Great Spirit came to him again: 'When thy people and Mine shall need to know My will, My spirit shall brood over thine and the words that thou shalt speak shall be My words.' Looking into the eager faces of longing and questioning, his spirit moved within him and he spoke:

'I went, I sought, I found the Great Spirit, who dwells in the earth as your spirits dwell in your bodies. It is from Him the spirit comes. We are His children. He cares for us more than a mother for the child at her breast, or the father for the son that is his pride. His love is like the air we breathe: it is about us; it is within us.

'The sun is the sign of His brightness, the sky of His greatness, and mother-love and father-love, and the love of man and woman are the signs of His love. We are but children; we cannot enter into the council of the Great Chief until we have been proved, but this is His will, that we love one another as He loves us; that we bury forever the hatchet of hate; that no man shall take what is not his own and the strong shall help the weak.'

The chiefs did not wholly understand the words of Wo, but they took a hatchet and buried it by the fire, saying: 'Thus bury we hate between man and his brother,' and they took an acorn and put it in the earth, saying: 'Thus plant we the love of the strong for the weak.' And it became the custom of the tribe that the great council in the spring should bury the hatchet and plant the acorn.

Every morning the tribe gathered to greet the rising sun, and, with right hands raised and left hands upon their hearts, prayed: 'Great Spirit, hear us; guide us today; make our wills Thy will, our ways Thy way.'

And the tribe grew stronger and greater and wiser than all the other tribes – but that is another story.

(Association Seminar, December 1910)

Bibliography

Camp-Fire Musings – William C. Gray. Fleming H. Revell Company. A book full of the spirit of the woods and of camp life.
Camp fire stories:
In Camp with Boys – G.W. Hinckley. Central Maine Pub. Co.
The Shadowless Man – Adelbert Von Chamisso. Frederick Warne & Co.
Mystery and Detective Stories, six volumes. Review of Reviews Co.

II

Tramps, Hikes and Overnight Trips

Afoot and light-hearted I take to the open road
Healthy, free, the world before me,
The long brown path before me leading wherever I choose.

(Whitman)

An Old Tramper's Advice

It is an excellent thing for the boys to get away from the camp routine for a few days, and walk 'the long brown path,' stopping overnight, doing their own cooking, building their 'lean-to' or shelter, and roughing it. Walking is probably one of the best all-round cures for the ills of civilisation. Several things should be remembered when one goes on a hike. First, avoid long distances. A foot-weary, muscle-tired, and temper-tried, hungry group of boys surely is not desirable. There are a lot of false notions about courage, and bravery, and grit, that read well in print but fail miserably in practice, and long hikes for boys is one of the most glaring of these notions. Second, have a leader who will set a good, easy pace, say about three miles an hour, prevent the boys from excessive water drinking, and assign the duties of pitching camp, etc. Third, observe these two rules given by an old woodsman: (1) Never walk over anything you can walk around; (2) Never step on anything that you can step over. Every time you step on anything you lift the weight of your body. Why lift extra weight when tramping? Fourth, carry with you only the things absolutely needed, and roll in blanket and poncho, army style.

Map Reading

Before starting on a hike, study carefully the road maps.

Shoe Wisdom

For tramping the boy needs the right kind of a shoe, or the trip will be a miserable failure. A light-soled or light-built shoe is not suited for mountain work, or even for an ordinary hike. The feet will blister and become 'road-weary'.

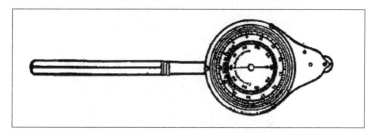

Above: Universal map measure

Right: Hiking pack

They must be neither too big nor too small nor too heavy, and be amply broad to give the toes plenty of room. The shoe should be water-tight. A medium weight, high-topped lace shoe is about right. Bathing the feet at the springs and streams along the road will be refreshing, if not indulged in too frequently. (See chapter on Health and Hygiene for care of the feet and proper way of walking).

It is well to carry a spare shirt hanging down the back with the sleeves tied round the neck. Change when the shirt you are wearing becomes too wet with perspiration.

The Pack

A few simple remedies for bruises, cuts, etc., should be taken along by the leader (see chapter on Simple Remedies). You may not need them, and some may poke fun at them, but as the old lady said: 'You can't always sometimes tell.' Amount and kind of provisions must be determined by the locality and habitation.

The 'Lean-to'

Reach the place where you are going to spend the night in plenty of time to build your 'lean-to', and make your bed for the night. Select your camping

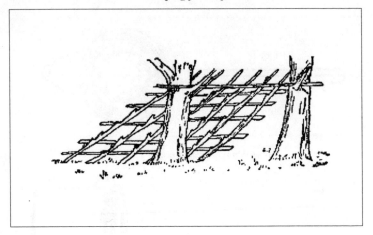

Frame of lean-to

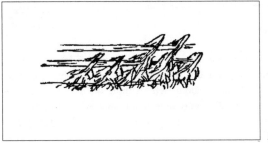

Method of thatching

spot, with reference to water, wood, drainage, and material for your 'lean-to.' Choose a dry, level place, the ground just sloping enough to insure the water running away from your 'lean-to' in case of rain. In building your 'lean-to,' look for a couple of good trees standing from eight to ten feet apart with branches from six to eight feet above the ground. By studying the illustration below, you will be able to build a very serviceable shack, affording protection from the dews and rain. While two or more boys are building the shack, another should be gathering firewood, and preparing the meal, while another should be cutting and bringing in as many soft, thick tips of hemlock or balsam boughs as possible, for the roof of the shack and the beds. How to thatch the 'lean-to' is shown in this illustration.

If the camp site is to be used for several days, two 'lean-tos' may be built facing each other, about six feet apart. This will make a very comfortable camp, as a small fire can be built between the two, thus giving warmth and light.

The Bed

On the floor of your 'lean-to' lay a thick layer of the 'fans' or branches of balsam fir or hemlock, with the convex side up, and the butts of the stems toward the foot of the bed. Now thatch this over with more 'fans' by thrusting the butt ends through the first layer at a slight angle toward the head of the bed, so that the soft tips will curve toward the foot of the bed, and be sure to make the head of your bed away from the opening of the 'lean-to' and the foot toward the opening. Over this bed spread your rubber blanket with rubber side down, your sleeping blanket on top, and you will be surprised how soft, springy, and fragrant a bed you have, upon which to rest your 'weary frame', and sing with the poet:

> Then the pine boughs croon me a lullaby,
>   And trickle the white moonbeams
> To my face on the balsam where I lie
>   While the owl hoots at my dreams.
>
> (J. George Frederick)

What God puts in the blood is eliminated slowly and we are all impregnated with a love for the natural life which is irresistible. That was a great saying of the boy who was taken from the city for the first time on an all-night outing. Snugly tucked up in his blankets he heard the wind singing in the pines overhead. As the boy looked up, he asked, 'Wasn't God blowing His breath down at us?'

(Dr Lilburn)

Hot Stones

If the night bids fair to be cold, place a number of stones about six or eight inches in diameter next the fire, so they will get hot. These can then be placed at the feet, back, etc., as needed, and will be found good 'bed warmers.' When a stone loses its heat it is replaced near the fire and a hot one is taken. If too hot, wrap the stone in a shirt or sweater or wait for it to cool off.

Night Watchers

Boys desire adventure. This desire may be gratified by the establishment of night watchers, in relays of two boys every two hours. Their imaginations will be stirred by the resistless attraction of the camp-fire and the sound of the creatures that creep at night.

Observation

Many boys have excellent eyes but see not, and good ears but hear not, all because they have not been trained to observe or to be quick to hear. A good method of teaching observation while on a hike or tramp is to have each boy jot down in a small notebook or diary of the trip the different kinds of trees, birds, animals, tracks, nature of roads, fences, peculiar rock formation, smells of plants, etc., and thus be able to tell what he saw or heard to the boys upon his return to the permanent camp or to his home.

Cameras

One of the party should take a Brownie No. 2 or small folding Kodak. Photos of the trip are always a great pleasure and a memory reviver. A practical and convenient method of carrying small folding cameras is described in *Forest and Stream*. A strap with a buckle having been attached to an ordinary leather belt is run through the loops at the back of the camera-case. The camera may be pushed around the belt to the point where it will be least in the way.

Lamps

A very convenient lamp to use on a hike is the Baldwin Camp Lamp. It weighs only five ounces when fully charged with carbide, and is but 4-3/4 inches high. It projects a strong light 150 feet through the woods. A stiff wind will not blow it out. It can be worn comfortably in your hat or belt.

The 'Rocky Mountain Searchlight', made of a discarded tomato can, a candle, and a bit of wire for a handle, is a camp product that will be found to be very useful in an emergency.

The can is carried lengthwise, with the wire handle run through a hole in the closed end on through the entire length of the can and out the open end. Do not wrap the handle wire around the can. It will slip off. Two cuts, crossing each other, make the candle opening, with the cut edges bent inward. The candle is pushed upward as it burns down, the flame being kept in the middle of the can. The cut edges prevent it from falling out until the last hold is melted away. The 'Searchlight' gives good service when hung in the tent or on a nearby tree, but is especially valuable in lighting up a rough path on a rainy, windy night.

The camp hanger shown in the illustration can be hung from the ridgepole of the tent, and is particularly useful when from two to four persons occupy the tent. It can be raised and lowered at will by attaching the hanger to a pulley arrangement. The hanger may be made of wood in any length. Ordinary coat hooks are fastened to the side with screws. A common screw-eye is used for the line at the top. A snap hook attached to the rope facilitates its removal at will.

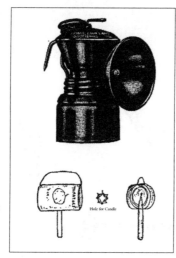

Right: Rocky
mountain lantern

Far right:
Camp hanger

A boy of ingenuity can make a number of convenient things. A good drinking cup may be made from a piece of birch bark cut in parallelogram shape, and twisted into pyramid form, and fastened with a split stick. (See illustrations on page 94.) A flat piece of bark may serve as a plate. A pot lifter may be made from a green stick about 18 inches long, allowing a few inches of a stout branch to remain. By reversing the same kind of stick and driving a small nail near the other end or cutting a notch, it may be used to suspend kettles over a fire. A novel candlestick is made by opening the blade of a knife and jabbing it into a tree, and upon the other upturned blade putting a candle. A green stick having a split end which will hold a piece of bread or meat makes an excellent broiler. Don't pierce the bread or meat. Driving a good-sized green stake into the ground at an angle of 45 degrees and cutting a notch in which may be suspended a kettle over the fire, will provide a way of boiling water quickly.

For suggestions in building a camp-fire and cooking on hikes, see chapter on Cooking on Hikes. The bibliography for the whole subject of Hikes, including cooking, is on page 99.

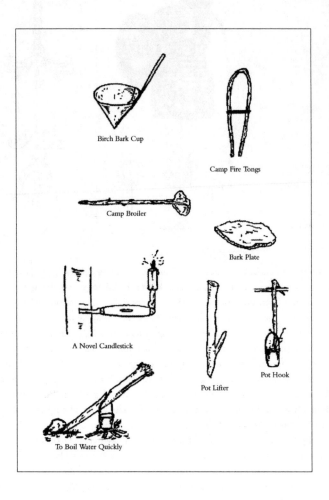

Birch Bark Cup

Camp Fire Tongs

Camp Broiler

Bark Plate

A Novel Candlestick

Pot Lifter

Pot Hook

To Boil Water Quickly

12

Cooking on Hikes

The Fireplace

Take two or three stones to build a fireplace; a stick first shaved and then whittled into shavings; a lighted match, a little blaze, some bark, dry twigs and a few small sticks added; then with the griddle placed over the fire, you are ready to cook the most appetising griddle cakes. After the cakes are cooked, fry strips of bacon upon the griddle; in the surplus fat fry slices of bread, then some thinly sliced raw potatoes done to a delicious brown and you have a breakfast capable of making the mouth of a camper water.

Another way of building a fire: Place two green logs side by side, closer together at one end than the other. Build fire between. On the logs over the fire you can rest frying pan, kettle, etc. To start fire, have some light, dry wood split up fine. When sticks begin to blaze add a few more of larger size and continue until you have a good fire.

Sun Glass

When the sun shines a fire may be started by means of a small pocket sun or magnifying glass. Fine scrapings from dry wood or 'punk tinder' will easily ignite by the focusing of the sun dial upon it, and by fanning the fire and by adding additional fuel, the fire-builder will soon have a great blaze.

Griddle Cakes

Beat together one egg, tablespoonful of sugar, cup of new milk, or condensed milk diluted one-half. Mix in enough self-raising flour to make a thick cream batter. Grease the griddle with rind or slices of bacon for each batch of cakes.

Broiled Bacon

Slice bacon thin. Remove the rind which makes the slices curl up. Or, gash the rind with a sharp knife if the boys like 'cracklings.' Fry on griddle or put on the sharp end of a stick and hold over the hot coals, or, better yet, remove the griddle and put a clean flat rock in its place. When the rock is hot lay the slices of bacon on it and broil. Keep turning the bacon so as to brown it on both sides. Cut into dice.

Creamed Salmon

Heat about a pint of salmon in one-half pint milk, season with salt and pepper and a half teaspoonful of butter.

Salmon on Toast

Drop slices of stale bread into smoking-hot lard. They will brown at once. Drain them. Heat a pint of salmon, picked into flakes, season with salt and pepper and put into it a tablespoonful of butter. Stir in one egg, beaten light, with three tablespoonfuls evaporated milk not thinned. Pour mixture on the fried bread.

Potatoes

Wash potatoes and dry well; bury them deep in a good bed of live coals, cover them with hot coals until well done. They will take about forty minutes to bake. When you can pass a sharpened hardwood sliver through them, they are done, and should be raked out at once. Run the sliver through them from end to end, and let the steam escape and use immediately, as a roast potato quickly becomes soggy and bitter.

Baked Fish

Dig a hole one foot and a half deep. Build a fire in it, heaping up dry sticks until there is an abundance of fuel. After an hour, take out the coals, clear the hole of ashes, lay green corn husks on the hot bottom of the hole. Soak brown paper in water and wrap around the fish. Lay it in the hole, cover with green corn husks, covered in turn with half an inch of earth. Build a fire over it and keep burning for an hour. Then remove and you have something delicious and worth the time taken to prepare.

Fried Fish

Clean fish well. Small fish should be fried whole, with the backbone severed to prevent curling up; large fish should be cut into pieces, and ribs cut loose from backbone so as to lie flat in pan. Rub the pieces in corn meal or powdered bread crumbs, thinly and evenly (that browns them). Fry in plenty of very hot fat to a golden brown, sprinkling lightly with pepper and salt just as the colour turns. If fish has not been wiped dry, it will absorb too much grease. If the frying fat is not very hot when fish are put in they will be soggy with it.

Frogs' Legs

After skinning frogs, soak them an hour in cold water, to which vinegar has been added, or put them for two minutes into scalding water that has vinegar in it. Drain, wipe dry, and cook. To fry: Roll in flour seasoned with salt and pepper, and fry, not too rapidly, preferably in butter or oil. Water cress is a good relish with them. To grill: Prepare three tablespoonfuls melted butter, one-half teaspoonful salt, and a pinch or two of pepper, into which dip the frog legs, then roll in fresh breadcrumbs and broil for three minutes on each side.

Eggs

Boiled: Raise water to boiling point. Place eggs in carefully. Boil steadily for three minutes if you prefer them soft. If you want them hard-boiled, put them in cold water, bring to a boil, and keep it up for twenty minutes. The yolk will then be mealy and wholesome.

Fried: Melt some butter or fat in frying pan, when it hisses drop in eggs carefully. Fry them three minutes.

Scrambled: First stir the eggs up with a little condensed cream and a pinch of salt and after putting some butter in the frying pan, stir the eggs in it, being careful not to cook them too long.

Poached: First put in the frying pan sufficient diluted condensed milk which has been thinned with enough water to float the eggs when the milk is hot; drop in the carefully opened eggs and let them simmer three or four minutes. Serve the eggs on slices of buttered toast, pouring on enough of the milk to moisten the toast.

Coffee

For every cup of water allow a tablespoonful of ground coffee, and one extra for the pot. Heat water to boiling point first, add coffee, boil five minutes, settle with one-fourth cup cold water and serve. Some prefer to put the coffee in a small muslin bag, tied loose, and boil for five minutes longer.

Cocoa

Allow a teaspoonful of cocoa for every cup of boiling water. Mix the powdered cocoa with hot water or hot milk to a creamy paste. Add equal parts of boiling water and boiled milk, and sugar to taste. Boil two or three minutes.

Sample Menu For an Overnight and a Day Hike or Tramp

Breakfast:
Griddle cakes with Karo Syrup or brown sugar and butter; fried bacon and potatoes; bread, coffee, preserves.

Dinner:
Creamed salmon on toast; baked potatoes; bread; pickles; fruit.

Supper:
Fried eggs; creamed or chipped beef; cheese; bread; cocoa.

These recipes have been tried out. Biscuit and bread-making have been purposely omitted. Take bread and crackers with you from the camp. 'Amateur' biscuits are not conducive to good digestion or happiness. Pack butter in a small jar. Cocoa, sugar and coffee in small cans or heavy paper, also salt and pepper. Wrap bread in a moist cloth to prevent drying up. Bacon and dried or chipped beef in wax paper. Pickles can be purchased put up in small bottles. Use the empty bottle as a candlestick.

Ration List for six boys, three meals

2 lbs. bacon (sliced thin),	3 cans salmon,
1 lb. butter,	24 potatoes,
1 doz. eggs,	2 cans condensed milk,
1/2 lb. cocoa,	1 small package self-raising flour,
1/2 lb. coffee,	Salt and pepper.
1 lb. sugar,	

Utensils

Small griddle or tin 'pie plate,'	Teaspoons,
Small stew pan,	Knives and forks,
Small coffee pot,	Plates and cups,
Small cake turner,	Matches and candles.
Large spoon,	

Dish Washing

First fill the frying pan with water, place over fire and let it boil. Pour out water and you will find that it has practically cleaned itself. Clean the griddle with sand and water. Greasy knives and forks may be cleaned by jabbing a couple of times into the ground. After all grease is gotten rid of, wash in hot water and dry with cloth. Don't use the cloth first and get it greasy.

Be sure to purchase Horace Kephart's excellent book on *Camp Cookery*, Outing Publishing Co., or Association Press. It is filled with practical suggestions.

Bibliography

Camp and Trail – Stewart Edward White. Doubleday, Page & Company. Full of common sense and of special value to those contemplating long tramps and wilderness travel. Several chapters on 'Horseback Travel.'

Out-of-Doors – M. Ellsworth Olsen, Ph.D. Pacific Press Publishing Co. A book permeated with a wholesome outdoor spirit.

The Field and Forest Book – Dan Beard. Charles Scribner's Sons. Written in 'Beardesque' style, filled with his inimitable illustrations and crammed with ideas.

The Way of the Woods-Edward Breck – G.P. Putnam's Sons. Simple, terse, free from technical terms, and calculated to give the novice a mass of information. Written for Northeastern United States and Canada, but of interest for every camper.

13

Health and Hygiene

Better to hunt on fields for health unbought
Than fee the doctor for a nauseous draught.
The wise, for cure, on exercise depend;
God never made his work for man to mend.

(Dryden)

Examination

A boy should be examined by his family physician before going to camp in order that he may receive the greatest good from the camp life and be safeguarded from physical excess. When the boy arrives in camp the physician or physical director examines the boy. Take his height, weight, lung capacity, condition of heart, lungs, condition of muscles, whether hard, medium or soft, and state of digestion. For this purpose you will need a wet spirometer, measuring rod, stethoscope and platform scales.

Give dates of first examination on arrival and final examination before departure from camp. The original is given to the boy to take home and the carbon copy is retained by the camp, filed in alphabetical order. Most remarkable gains have been made by boys, particularly in lung capacity, height, and hardening of muscles. The active life of the camp is not conducive as a rule to great gain in weight.

Each tent leader should be given the important facts of the examinations of the boys in his tent, so that there may be intelligent cooperation between the physician, or physical director, the tent leader, and the boy in securing health efficiency.

Average physical types for boys of 5 to 16 years.
(Compiled from the measurements of 5,476 school children.)

Age	Weight	Height	Height sitting	Span of arms	Breadth head	Breadth chest	Breadth waist
16	116.38	64.45	33.55	66.25	5.95	9.85	9.15
15	103.29	62.25	32.15	63.15	5.90	9.30	8.65
14	87.41	59.45	30.70	60.00	5.85	8.95	8.25
13	78.32	57.10	29.60	57.50	5.80	8.70	7.95
12	72.55	55.25	28.95	55.30	5.80	8.50	7.70
11	64.89	53.10	28.20	53.40	5.75	8.25	7.45
10	61.28	51.55	27.60	51.20	5.75	8.00	7.20
9	55.15	49.55	26.80	49.10	5.70	7.80	7.10
8	50.90	47.75	26.00	47.00	5.65	7.65	6.95
7	46.85	45.55	25.20	45.00	5.65	7.45	6.75
6	42.62	43.55	24.20	42.60	5.60	7.25	6.55
5	39.29	41.60	23.30	40.35	5.60	7.15	6.50

Age	Girth			Strength			
	Chest depth	Girth of head	Chest expansion	Lung capacity (cu in)	Right fore-arm strength	Left forearm strength	Vitality coefficient
16	6.60	21.55	3.45	191.40	73.28	65.22	35.58
15	6.30	21.45	3.30	161.00	63.47	54.30	26.09
14	5.95	21.30	3.35	140.12	55.81	50.70	21.97
13	5.65	21.10	3.25	123.58	49.69	45.07	18.28

12	5.60	21.00	3.05	111.33	43.29	40.56	15.55
11	5.45	20.85	2.90	100.74	39.09	36.30	13.33
10	5.25	20.60	2.75	90.02	32.42	30.94	10.84
9	5.20	20.65	2.55	81.03	28.91	25.90	9.34
8	5.10	20.55	2.35	70.43	23.38	20.96	7.34
7	5.10	20.45	1.80	60.48	20.19	18.78	5.05
6	5.05	20.25	1.65	50.89	15.36	12.53	4.02
5	4.90	20.15	1.35	40.60	10.76	10.38	2.62

Copyright by Wm. W. Hastings, Ph.D.

Hospital Tent

If a boy is ill (minor aches and pains which are frequently only growing pains, excepted), isolate him from the camp, so that he may have quiet and receive careful attention.

A tent, with fly and board floor, known as the 'Hospital Tent' or 'Red Cross Tent', should be a part of the camp equipment. There may be no occasion for its use, but it should be ready for any emergency. The physician may have his office in this tent. Boys should not be 'coddled'; at the same time it must not be forgotten that good, sympathetic attention and nursing are two-thirds responsible for speedy recovery from most ills.

Equipment

A spring cot, mattress, pillow, blankets, a good medicine cabinet, alcohol stove for boiling water, cooking food, and sterilising instruments; pans, white enamelled slop jar, pitcher, cup, pail; a table, a folding camp reclining chair (Gold Medal Camp Furniture Company), and a combination camp cot and litter (Gold Medal Brand) will make up the equipment of the tent.

The information and suggestions given in this chapter are the accumulation of many years' experience in boys' camps. The technical information is vouched for by competent physicians who have examined the manuscript.[1]

Pulse Rate

Every man in charge of a boys' camp should have a knowledge of certain physiological facts, so as to be able to make a fair diagnosis of pain and disease. The pulse, taken at the wrist, is a fair index of the condition of the body. In taking the pulse-beat, do so with the fingers, and not with the thumb, as the beating of the artery in the thumb may confuse. Pulse rate is modified with age, rest, exercise, position, excitements, and elevation. High elevation produces a more rapid pulse. The normal rate of boys in their teens is about 80 to 84 beats per minute. An increase not accounted for by one of the above reasons usually means fever, a rise of 6 beats in pulse usually being equivalent to a rise of 1 degree. Often more important than the rate, however, is the quality of the pulse. Roughly, the feebler the pulse, the more serious the condition of the individual. Irregularity in the rate may be a serious sign, and when it is noticed a doctor should be immediately called. Failure to find the artery should not necessarily cause uneasiness, as by trying on himself, the director may see that the taking of the pulse is often a difficult undertaking.

The Tongue

The tongue is a very misleading guide to the patient's condition, and no definite rule about its appearance can be laid down. Other signs, such as temperature, general conditions, localisation of pain, etc., are more accurate, and to the total result of such observations the appearance of the tongue adds little.

Thermometer

The normal temperature of the human body by mouth is about 98.4 degrees. Variations between 98 degrees and 99 degrees are not necessarily significant of disease. A reliable clinical thermometer should be used. Temperature is generally taken in the mouth. Insert the bulb of the thermometer well under the boy's tongue. Tell him to close his lips, not his teeth, and to breathe through his nose. Leave it in the mouth about three or four minutes. Remove, and, after noting temperature, rinse it in cold water, dry it with a clean, towel, and shake the mercury down to 95 degrees. It will then be ready for use next time. Never return a thermometer to its case unwashed.

Pain

Pain is an indication that there is something wrong with the body that should receive attention. Some boys are more sensitive to pain than others, particularly boys of a highly strung, delicate, nervous nature. Most people, however, think too much of their pains. Most pains to which boys fall heir are due to trouble in the stomach or intestines, or to fevers. Many pains that boys feel mean very little. They are often due to a sore or strained muscle or nerve. A hot application or massage will often bring relief.

Sharply localised pain, except as the result of external injury, is not common among healthy boys, and, if found, particularly in the well-known appendix area, and if accompanied by other disquieting signs (temperature, pulse, etc.), should receive medical attention.

In a general way, any abdominal pain that does not yield in 24 hours to rest in bed with application of external heat, should call for the advice of a physician. Any severe attack of vomiting or diarrhoea, accompanied by temperature, and not immediately traceable to some indiscretion in diet, is cause for study, and if improvement does not soon show itself, a physician should be called.

Pains in the extremities, particularly joints, if not clearly showing signs of improvement in two or three days, should also be the object of a physician's visit, as a fracture near a joint, if not correctly treated early, may result in permanent deformity.

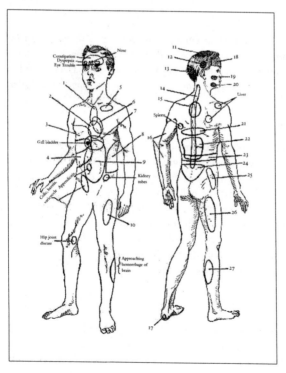

Sites of pain

The camp physician, or director, if he himself assumes the medical responsibilities, should enforce the rule that all boys who do not have a daily movement of the bowels see him, and he should always be ready to receive such cases and give them the necessary treatment.

The drawings by Albert G. Wegener illustrate in a general way what the trouble is when one feels a distinct, persistent pain.

Among healthy boys, in camp, thoracic pains, other than those due to muscular strain, are uncommon, but when severe, especially if accompanied by a rise of temperature (over 99.5 degrees) and not readily succumbing to rest in bed, should be investigated by a physician.

Pain

The accompanying diagrams indicate what ailment may be looked for if there is a persistent pain. (Adapted from Butler; Diagnosis).

1 Disease of bone. Tumour or abscess in chest. Weakening of the aorta. Stomach trouble.
2 Catarrh,[2] or cancer or ulcer of stomach. Disease of spinal column. Inflammation of pancreas.
3 Lack of blood. Neuralgia of rib nerves. Pneumonia. Enlarged glands. Disease of chest wall. Disease of back-bone. Shingles.
4 Liver disease. Weakness of abdominal aorta. Heart disease.
5 Disease of diaphragm or large intestines.
6 Heart disease. Large intestines. Locomotor ataxia.[3]
7 Pleurisy. Violent vomiting. Coughing.
8 Colic. Gravel. Movable kidney. Enlarged spleen. Dyspepsia. Lack of blood. Debility.
9 Sharp abdominal pains indicate the following: Ulcer or cancer of stomach. Disease of intestines. Lead colic. Arsenic or mercury poisoning. Floating kidney. Gas in intestines. Clogged intestines. Appendicitis. Inflammation of bowels. Rheumatism of bowels. Hernia. Locomotor ataxia. Pneumonia. Diabetes.
10 Neuralgia. Clogged intestines. Abdominal tumour. Kidney colic. Tumour or abscess of thigh bone. Appendicitis if pain is in right leg.
11 Lack of blood. Hysteria. Epilepsy. Disease of bladder. Nervous breakdown.
12 Foreign substance in ear. Bad teeth. Eye strain. Disease of Jaw bone. Ulcer of tongue.
13 Nervous breakdown. Epilepsy. Tumour or break in brain. Cranial neuralgia. Disease of neck bones. Adenoids. Ear disease. Eye strain. Bad teeth.
14 Spinal trouble.
15 Disease of stomach. Weakening of aorta.

16 Hand and arm pains indicate: Heart disease. Enlarged spleen. Clogged large intestines.
17 Nervous breakdown.
18 Eye strain. Disease of nasal cavity. Lack of blood. Dyspepsia. Constipation. Rheumatism of scalp. Nervous breakdown.
19 Bad teeth. Ear inflammation. Cancer of upper Jaw. Neuralgia of Jaw nerve.
20 Bad teeth. Neuralgia of Jaw nerve.
21 Clogged large intestines. Ulcer of stomach.
22 Lumbago. Neuralgia. Debility. Fatigue. Weakness of abdominal aorta.
23 Girdle sensation indicates disease or injury of spinal cord.
24 Disease of testicles. Excessive sex abuse. Ulcer or cancer rectum. Piles. Disease of hip-joint. Neuralgia. Sciatica.
25 Kidney disease. Neuralgia.
26 Intestines clogged. Cancer or ulcer of rectum. Locomotor ataxia. Abscess in back. Sciatica (if in one leg only).
27 Cramps due to over exercise. Diabetes. Hysteria.

Typhoid Fever

The epidemic chiefly to be feared in summer camps is typhoid fever, and boys coming from cities where that disease is prevalent should be carefully watched. Care in sanitation minimises the likelihood of such a disease springing up in the camp. Other infections, such as mumps, conjunctivitis, etc., should be carefully isolated, and all precautions taken to prevent their spread.

A fairly common event may be toward evening to find a boy with a headache and a temperature perhaps of 102 degrees. This will probably be all right in the morning after a night's rest and perhaps the administration also of a cathartic.

The Dentist

The importance of a visit to the dentist before coming to camp cannot be over-estimated. Everyone knows the torture of a toothache, and realises how unbearable it must be for a boy away from home and among other boys, sympathetic, of course, but busy having a good time, and with only a few patent gums to relieve the misery, and the dentist perhaps not available for two days. Parents cannot have this point too forcibly thrust upon them, as by even a single visit to a competent dentist all the sufferings of toothache may usually be prevented.

Surgical Supplies

The following list of surgical supplies will be found necessary. The quantity must be determined by the size of the camp, and the price by the firm from whom purchased:

One-half dozen assorted gauze bandages, sizes one to three inches.
Two yards sterilised plain gauze in carton.
One roll three-inch adhesive plaster.
One paper medium size safety pins.
One paper medium size common pins.
Four ounces sterilised absorbent cotton in cartons.
One-half dozen assorted egg-eyed surgeon's needles, straight to full curve.
One card braided silk ligature, assorted in one card (white).
One hundred ordinary corrosive sublimate tablets.
Small surgical instrument set, comprising of 2 scalpels, forceps, director, probe, curette, scissors.
One Hypodermic Syringe, all metal, in metal case.
One Fountain Syringe (for enemata and ears).
One one-minute clinical thermometer in rubber case. Get best registered instrument.
One number nine soft rubber catheter.
Small bottle collodion[4] with brush.
One-quarter pound Boric acid powder.
Four ounces Boric acid ointment.
One-quarter pound Boric acid crystals. Carbolic Acid.
Hypodermic tablets, cocaine hydro-chlorate, 1-1/8 grain, making in two drachms sterile water or one per cent solution. (To be used by Physician only.)
Alcohol, 80 per cent.
Sulpho Napthol.
Iodoform gauze.
Chloroform liniment.

With the above list the ingenious man can perform practically every surgical operation that he would care to undertake.

For 'First Aid' demonstration work you will need a number of Red Cross Outfits.

Medical Store

(Tablets to be used hypodermically should be used only by a physician.)

Quinine Sulphate, gr. 5. Useful in malarial regions. Give 15-20 gr. At time of expected chill. Better stay away from malarial country. No place for a camp.

Calomel, gr. 1/4. Take one tablet every 30 minutes or every hour, for eight doses in all cases where bowels need thorough cleaning out.

Phenacetine and *Salol*, of each gr. 2-1/2. One tablet every four hours. For headache and intestinal antisepsis. Dangerous as a depressant to heart.

Dover's Powders, gr. 5. Two tablets at bedtime, in hot water or lemonade, in acute colds. One after each meal may be added.

Dobell's Solution Tablets. One as a gargle in one-half glass hot water every two to four hours in tonsillitis and pharyngitis.

Potassium Bromide, gr. 10. For headache. Best given in solution after meals. May irritate an empty stomach.

Aspirin, gr. 5. One or two every four hours for rheumatism, headache, or general pains and aches.

Compound cathartic pills. Two at night for constipation.

Epsom Salts, four ounces. Two to four teaspoonfuls in hot water before breakfast.

Compound tincture of opium (Squibb), 4 ounces. Teaspoonful after meals for summer diarrhoea.

Baking soda. Teaspoonful after meals for 'distress'.

Morphine Sulphate, gr. 1/4;

Strychnine Sulphate, gr. 1-30; for hypodermics, used by physicians only.

In addition to the above everyone has a stock of 'old-fashioned' home remedies. Some of these are described under 'Simple Remedies'.

Bibliography

Backwoods Surgery and Medicine – Charles Stuart Moody, M.D. Outing Publishing Co., New York. A commonsense book written from experience. It is invaluable to campers.

Home Treatment and Care of the Sick – A. Temple Lovering, M.D. Otis Clapp & Son, Boston. Full of helpful suggestions.

Boys' Drill Regulations – National First Aid Association, 6 Beacon Street, Boston, Mass. A mass of information concerning setting-up drills, litter drills, swimming drill on land, rescue and resuscitation drills, etc.

14

Simple Remedies

In a small camp a physician is unnecessary, though one should be within call. The camp leader should have a knowledge of the ordinary ailments of growing boys and simple remedies for relief. No camp of fifty or more boys should be without a physician or some upper class medical student of high moral character. Don't run risks. When in doubt, call in a physician. The treatment of local disorders described is largely from nature's medicine chest, and simple in application.

Bites and Stings

Put on salt and water, or make a paste of soda and water, or rub the wound with aromatic ammonia, camphor, or tar soap. Common salt is excellent.

Bleeding Nose

Do not blow the nose. Hold a wet handkerchief at the back of the neck and wash the face in hot water, or place a wad of paper under the upper lip, or crowd some fine gauze or cotton into the nostrils and make a plug.

To Check Bleeding

Raise the injured part as high as you can above the heart, press very firmly with sterile pad under thumb or fingers on or into the wound. Blood from a vein will be dark red or purplish and will flow in a steady stream. Press upon the vein below the wound. Put on a clean pad and bind it upon the wound firmly enough to stop bleeding. Blood from an artery will be bright red and will probably spurt in jets. Press very hard above the wound. Tie a strong bandage (handkerchief, belt, suspenders, rope, strip of clothing) around the wounded member, and between the wound and the heart. Under it and directly over the artery place a smooth pebble, piece of stick, or other hard lump. Then thrust a stout stick under the bandage and twist until the wound stops bleeding. A tourniquet should not remain over twenty-four hours.

Blisters

Wash blistered feet in hot water and then in alcohol or in cold water with a little baking powder or soda added. Wipe them dry and then rub them with a tallow candle or some fat.

Bruises

Apply compresses of hot or cold water to keep down swelling and discolouration. Also apply witch hazel.

Burns

Use Vaseline, baking soda, bread, the white of an egg, flour and water, butter, grease, or fat; or mix flour and soda with fat, or soap with sugar and make into a paste, or put a teaspoonful of baking powder into a pint of warm water and pour it on a piece of gauze and put this on the burn or scald, covering it with cotton and a bandage. Never let a burn be exposed to the air, but cover it at once if the pain is intense.

Chills

Mix a good dash of pepper with a little ginger in sweetened hot water and drink it. Get into bed at once. Cover with blankets and put hot water bottle at feet.

Choking

Force yourself to swallow pieces of dry bread or drink some water. Let some one slap the back.

Colds

Pour boiling water over two heads of elder blossoms, brew for twenty minutes, and drink a small cup hot on going to bed. Or drink hot lemonade or hot ginger tea. In any case, keep warm and out of a draft.

Constipation

Use cathartic pills, or castor oil. Eat plenty of prunes or fruit. Drink plenty of water.

Cuts

Always clean thoroughly all open wounds to prevent infection, and accelerate healing. Carbolic, left on a wound for any time at all may result in carbolic poisoning or in gangrene. Use pure alcohol (not wood or denatured, as both are poisonous), or a teaspoonful of sulphur-naphthol to a basin of water, or 1:1,000 corrosive sublimate solution (wad with flexible collodion). Do not use Vaseline or any other substance on a freshly abrased surface. After a scab has formed, Vaseline may be applied to keep this scab soft. Never close a wound with court plaster.[1] The only legitimate uses for sticking or adhesive plaster are to hold dressings in place where bandaging is difficult, or in case of a cut to keep edges closed without sewing the skin.

Earache

Take the heart of an onion, heat it in an oven, and put it in the ear when hot, but not so hot as to burn the ear. This not only relieves the earache, but helps to send the sufferer to sleep. Hold hot water bag to ear.

Inflamed Eye

Wring a towel in water hot as the hands will bear; lay on the eyes and change frequently. Bathe with saturated solution of boric acid crystals.

Great relief is felt by opening the eyes in tepid or very warm boracic solution. Even if it is strong enough to smart, no harm will result.

If inflammation is caused by a foreign substance, rub the other eye, in order to make both eyes water. If the speck can be seen, it can generally be taken out by twisting a small piece of gauze or cloth around a toothpick and drawing it over the speck, or by twisting up a piece of paper like a lamp lighter and, after wetting the tip of it, wiping it against the speck. If it is under the upper lid, pull the lid away from the eyeball, and push the under lid up underneath the upper one. In this way the eyelashes of the lower lid will generally clean the inside of the upper one. An eye-tweezers for removing a piece of grit from the eye is made by folding a piece of paper in two. With a sharp knife cut it to a point at an angle of 30 degrees and slightly moisten the point in clean water.

Feet

It is a good thing to dry-soap your feet and the inside of your socks before putting them on for a hike or tramp. This is an old army trick. If your feet perspire freely, powder them with boric acid powder, starch, and oxide of zinc in equal parts. Wash the feet every day, best on turning in at night.

To prevent the nail growing into the toe, take a bit of broken glass and scrape down the top of the nail until it is quite thin, and in time the corners begin to grow out, and no longer hurt the toe. Toenails should be cut square and not encouraged to grow in by side trimming. A good plan is to make a 'V' shape notch on the middle of the top of each toenail, which will close up naturally, and, in so doing, draw the sides up and inward.

Headache

Headache comes from indigestion or from the sun. A boy will overeat and then play under the hot sun – result, headache. Have the boy lie down and sleep, if possible, using cloths dipped in cold water to drive the blood away from the head. A remedy recommended by the great John Wesley is to lay very thin slices of lemon rind on either temple.

Hiccough

Take a deep breath and hold it as long as possible, or make yourself sneeze.

Ivy Poisoning

Mix some baking powder with water, or rub on wood ashes. Wash with alcohol. Be careful not to spread by scratching.

Rusty Nail

Better call a physician. Puncture with nails and such things, especially if rusty, should be squeezed and washed with sulphur-naphthol or hot water poured into the hole. If too small, this may be slightly enlarged. Cauterise with carbolic acid, then with pure alcohol. Keep the wound open for a few days. Run no risk with a rusty nail wound. Attend to it immediately.

Sprains

Bathe a sprain in as hot water as you can bear, to which has been added a small quantity of vinegar and salt. Slight sprains (as of finger) may be painted with iodine.

Sunstroke

The first symptom is a headache followed by a heavy feeling in the pit of the stomach, dimmed eyesight, difficulty in breathing, and a fever. If insensibility follows, lay the person on his back in a cool, shady place, with his head slightly raised. Loosen his clothing, keep his head cold with wet cloths, and pour cold water on his face and chest, until the temperature of his body is lowered and the face becomes pale.

Sunburn

Get used to sun gradually. Use powdered boric acid or ointment. Cocoa butter is also a good preventive.

Sore Throat

Gargle the throat with warm water and some salt added, and then bind a woollen sock around it. Keep the sock on until the soreness is gone. Put a teaspoonful of chlorate of potash in a cup of water and gargle. Diluted alkalol [sic] is also good for a gargle, or tincture of iron diluted. Fat bacon or pork may be tied around the neck with a dry sock. Swab the throat.

Stomach ache

Caused by undigested food in the intestines. Put the boy on a diet, also give him plenty of warm water to drink, or a cup of hot ginger tea.

Toothache

Heat will always help to soothe the sufferer. A seeded raisin, toasted before the fire, makes a useful poultice for an aching tooth, pressed into the hollow. A bag of hot salt, pressed on the face, relieves pain.

15

First Aid

First aid should teach every boy how to render temporary assistance by improvised means for the relief of the injured one, and the methods by which he can be removed to a place of safety. With this in view, the information given in this chapter incorporates what every camper should know. Before going to camp, boys should be taught the use of the Triangular Bandage. This bandage is well suited for an emergency bandage. It can be easily made from a handkerchief or a piece of linen. The gauze or roller bandage is more difficult to handle. This, however, is the bandage to control bleeding, etc. Any reliable book on First Aid gives information as to its manipulation.

Dislocation

A dislocation of the finger or toe can generally be reduced by pulling strongly and at the same time pressing where the dislocation is. If the hip, shoulder, or elbow is dislocated, do not meddle with the joint, but make the boy as comfortable as possible by surrounding the joint with flannel cloths wrung out in hot water; support with soft pads, and send for a doctor at once. If the spine is dislocated, lay the boy on his back. Never put him on his side or face, it may be fatal. If he is cold, apply hot blankets to his body, hot water bottle or hot salt bag to the seat of pain.

Broken Bones

Do not try to reduce the fracture if a physician can be secured, for unskilled handling will do more harm than good. The thing to do is to make the boy comfortable by placing him in a comfortable position with the injured part resting on a pad, keeping him perfectly quiet. If there is an open wound, cover it with cheesecloth or gauze which has been dipped in boiling water, to which baking soda has been added. Then wrap absorbent cotton around it. If the boy has a fever, put wet cloths on his head, swinging them in the air to cool for changing.

The following practical suggestions are given in *Camp kits and camp life*, by Charles Stedman Hanks:

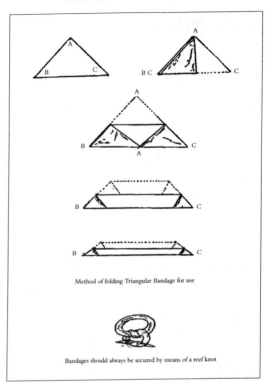

Method of folding Triangular Bandage for use

Triangular bandage; method of folding triangular bandage for use; bandage should always be secured by means of a reef knot

Bandages should always be secured by means of a reef knot

Nose

If the nose is broken, plug with gauze to stop bleeding.

Jaw

If the jaw is broken, push the bone gently into place, and if there is an open wound, cover it with gauze or cotton, made antiseptically, and then put a bandage around the jaw.

Collar Bone

If the collar bone is broken, it will be known by the pain in the shoulder and the shoulder dropping. Holding the elbow up will relieve the weight from the collar bone. Lay the boy on his back. Put a cotton wad in his armpit and bandage the arm to the side of the body and put the arm in a sling.

Shoulder Blade

If the shoulder blade is broken, put the forearm across the chest with the fingers on the shoulder and then bandage the arm to the body.

Rib

If a rib is broken it will pain the patient when he takes a long breath. Put him on his back, resting a little on the uninjured side, so that he will breathe easily. If it is necessary to move him, bandage strips of adhesive plaster around the body, beginning at the lowest rib and working upward, having each strip lap over the one below it. If you have no adhesive plaster, use a wide strip of cotton cloth. After you have put his coat on, pin it as tightly as you can in the back.

Leg Above Knee

If the leg is broken above the knee, lay shoulders slightly back, with the head and shoulders slightly raised. Draw the leg out straight, and, after padding it with cotton or towels, cut a small sapling long enough to reach from the foot to the armpit, and fasten it at the ankle, knee, and waist. If it is necessary to move the boy, bind both legs firmly together.

Leg Below Knee

If the leg is broken below the knee, lay the boy on his back and put a pillow or a bag stuffed with grass lengthwise under it. Then put a board or a hewed sapling on the under side of the pillow to stiffen it, and bandage the pillow and the board or sapling firmly to the leg. If the boy has to be moved, bind both legs together.

Knee Pan

If the knee pan is broken, put the boy on his back and straighten out the leg on a padded splint which reaches from the heel to the hip, putting some cotton or a folded towel under the knee and the heel. Then bandage the splint on at the ankle, at the upper part of the leg, and above and below the knee pan.

Foot

If the foot is broken, make a splint of two pieces of wood held together at right angles, and, after padding the foot with cotton, bind the splint to the side of the foot and the leg.

Above left: Large arm sling as a support for the forearm

Above right: Large arm sling as a support for the elbow

Upper Arm

If the upper arm is broken, make three splints, one long enough to reach from the shoulder to the elbow to go on the outside of the arm, one to go on the inner side of the arm, and one on the back of the arm. Pad the arm from the armpit to the elbow with cotton, towels, or newspapers wrapped in cloth, and, after bandaging on the splints, put the forearm in a sling and bind the arm to the body.

Forearm

If the forearm is broken, make a cotton pad long enough to reach from the fingers well up to the forearm, and rest the palm of the hand on it. Put a similar pad on the back of the hand, and, after bandaging in a splint, put the arm in a sling.

Hand

If the hand is broken, put a cotton pad on the palm and over it a thin splint long enough to reach from the tips of the fingers to the forearm. After binding the splint in place, put the arm in a sling with the hand higher than the elbow.

Finger

If a finger is broken, make a splint of cardboard or a thin piece of wood long enough to reach from the tip of the finger to the wrist. Cover the finger with gauze or cotton, and, after binding on the splint, support the hand in a sling.

Fainting

Fainting comes from too little blood in the head. Lay the boy on his back with feet higher than his head. Loosen tight clothing and let him have plenty of fresh air. Sprinkle his face with cold water and rub his arms with it. For an attack of dizziness, bend the head down firmly between the knees. If his face is flushed, raise the head.

Stunned

Lay the boy on his back with head somewhat raised. Apply heat, such as bottles of hot water, hot plates or stones wrapped in towels to the extremities and over the stomach, but keep the head cool with wet cloths. Do not give any stimulant; it would drive blood to the brain.

Stretcher

A stretcher may be improvised in one of the following ways:

(a) A shutter, door, or gate covered well with straw, hay, clothing, or burlap bagging.
(b) A piece of carpet, blanket, sacking, tarlatan, spread out, and two stout poles rolled up in the sides. Put clothes for a pillow.
(c) A coat with the two sleeves turned inside out; pass two poles through the sleeves, button the coat over them. (See illustration below.) Patient sits on coat and rests against the back of the first bearer.
(d) Two poles passed through a couple of bags, through holes at bottom corners of each.

Carry a patient by walking out of step, and take short paces, about 18 inches apart. Usually carry the patient feet first, but in going up hill the position is reversed, and the patient is carried head first.

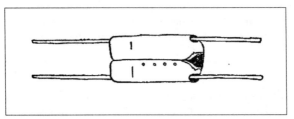

Coat stretcher

The following illustrations explain the process of carrying a patient without a stretcher:

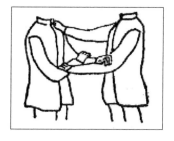

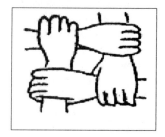

Above left: Three-handed seat

Above right: Four-handed seat

Prevention from drowning

Learn to Swim
Every summer records its hundreds of drowning accidents, many of which might have been prevented if methods of rescue had been generally taught. No boy should be permitted to enter a boat, particularly a canoe, until he has learned to swim. The movement to teach swimming to every boy and young man who does not know how to swim is both commendable and practical. The text-book used largely is *At Home in the Water*, by George H. Corsan, issued by the publishers of this book.

Button Awards
Summer camps provide a special opportunity for giving such instruction. To each individual who is actually taught to swim in camp a silver-oxidized button is given provided the test is made under the supervision of a committee of three men. Those who teach others to swim receive a gold oxidized leader's button.

Life Saving Corps
An Auxiliary Division of the Life Saving Corps should be established to patrol the water during swimming periods. Any camper may qualify for member-ship by taking the following examinations: the boy to receive not less than 6 points in 10 point subjects, and not less than 3 points on 5 point subjects, with a total of 75 points. Those receiving less than 75 points may become members of auxiliary crews.

How to qualify

1 Swimming not less than 100 yards and 25 yards on back. 10 points
2 Diving, plunging, floating, fetching. 10 points
3 Rescue drill on land and water. 10 points
4 Release drill on land and in water. 10 points
5 Resuscitation. 10 points
6 Names of parts of a row boat. 5 points
7 Rowing and boat handling. 10 points
8 Use of life saving appliances. 10 points
9 First aid work and remedies. 10 points
10 Written examination on work in water. 5 points
11 Written examination on work in boats. 5 points
12 Written examination on work on land. 5 points

Organisation

To organise at camps, officials will proceed by conducting the above-mentioned examinations. Should there be five or more successful competitors, crews can be organised as follows, the regular form of enrolment being employed and no enlistments required:

Five men constitute a crew entitling one of the five to the rank of acting third lieutenant.

Ten men constitute two crews with acting second and third lieutenants.

Fifteen men constitute three crews with acting first, second, and third lieutenants.

Twenty men constitute four crews (or a division) with acting captain, first, second, and third lieutenants, lieutenant surgeon, quartermaster, boatswain, and one coxswain for each crew or three coxswains.

Auxiliary members over eighteen years of age may become active members after leaving camps and receive active membership commissions, provided they affiliate with some active permanent crew in their home district.

Auxiliary members holding our certificates shall be entitled to auxiliary membership buttons, but active members only are entitled to wear the official badge of membership of the corps.

Summer camps will be equipped, at the discretion of headquarters, on the following conditions:

That they shall pay all express on supplies to and from camps.

That they shall report at the end of each season the exact condition of the supplies and make provision for the safekeeping of same for future seasons, or return same.

Medicine chests must be returned.

Instructors will be sent to the various camps, at the discretion of headquarters, whenever possible. All expenses, travelling, board, etc., but not services, must be covered by the camps.

Examination questions will be found in our book, *Instruction on Subjects for Examination for Membership*. If desired, camp officials can make examinations more rigid than outlined by us.

Examination papers furnished on request.

Training Course

Efficient life saving comes from thorough experience and training, not from a theory. These subjects for instruction may be taught preparatory to the summer camp, as well as during the camping season.

Swimming to include straight-away, swimming with clothes on, floating, diving, fetching: strokes – perfect breast stroke, side stroke, overhead stroke, crawl stroke.

Rescue Methods to include rescuing a supposedly drowning person. Use of life saving apparatus.

Methods of Release to include grasping by the wrist, clutch around the neck and grasp around the body.

Resuscitation of the apparently drowned, including the Sylvester method described on page 194, and the simple 'first aid' rules.

Boat Handling to include rowing a boat, taking a person into a boat from the water, clinging to a boat without capsizing it, etc.

Knot Tying to include all kinds of knots and their value in connection with life-saving work, and the use of them on life-saving appliances.

Wig-Wag code

Signalling by wig-wag is carried on by waving a flag in certain ways, represented by the illustration overleaf, and thus letters are made and words spelled.

Two wig-wag flags are used, one a square white flag with a red square in the centre, and the other a square red flag with white square in the centre.

Only one flag is used in signalling, and that one is selected which can best be seen against the boy's background.

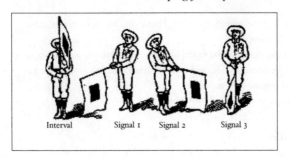

| Interval | Signal 1 | Signal 2 | Signal 3 |

Wig-Wag signal code

Alphabet:

A	22	G	2211	N	11	U	112
B	2122	H	122	O	21	V	1222
C	121	I	1	P	121	W	1121
D	222	J	1122	Q	1211	X	2122
E	12	K	2121	R	211	Y	111
F	2221	L	221	S	212	Z	2222
		M	1221	T	2	tion	1112

Alphabet classified:

I 1	**E** 12	**C** 121	**T** 2	**O** 21	**S** 212
N 11	**H** 122	**Q** 1211	**A** 22	**R** 211	**X** 2122
Y 111	**V** 1222	**M** 1221	**D** 222	**L** 221	**B** 2112
	U 112	**P** 1212	**Z** 2222	**G** 2211	**K** 2121
	J 1122	**W** 1121		**F** 2221	

Numerals:

1 1111	**3** 1112	**5** 1122	**7** 1222	**9** 1221
2 2222	**4** 2221	**6** 2211	**8** 2111	**0** 2112

Conventional signals:
End of word, 3
End of sentence, 33
End of message, 333
I understand, A.A. 3
Cease signalling, A.A.A. 333
Repeat last word, C.C. 3
Repeat last message, C.C.C. 3
I have made an error, E.E. 3

Wig-wag Rules

1   The boy should face the person to whom he is signalling, and should hold the flag-staff vertically in front of the centre of his body, with the butt at the height of his waist.
2   The motion represented by the Figure 1 is made by waving the flag down to the right; 2, by waving it down to the left; and 3, by waving it down in front of the sender. (Page 122)
3   Each motion should embrace an arc of ninety degrees, starting from and returning to the vertical without a pause.
4   When two or more motions are required to make a letter, there should be no pause between the motions.
5   At the end of each letter there should be a slight pause at the vertical.
6   At the end of each word, one front motion (3) should be made; at the end of a sentence, two fronts (33); and at the end of a message, three fronts (333).
7   To call a boat, signal the initial letter of her name until answered. To answer a call, signal A.A. 3 (I understand).
8   If the sender makes an error he should immediately signal E.E. 3 (I have made an error), and resume the message, beginning with the last word sent correctly.
9   If the receiver does not understand a signal he should signal C.C. 3 (Repeat last word); the sender should then repeat the last word and proceed with the message.

Examination example, 24 August 1910:

A – Boat Work – 10 Points

1   With what knot should you tie a boat?
2   Define amidships, thole-pin,[1] painter.[2]
3   Define port, starboard, aft.
4   Explain briefly a rescue from the bow.
5   Explain briefly a rescue from the stern.

B – Water Work – 10 Points

1 Describe breakaway Number 3.
2 'Before jumping into water for rescue, be sure to do –' what?
3 Give two ways to locate a body.
4 If you are seized and cannot break away, what should you do?
5 'If in a strong out setting tide, it is advisable when rescuing to –' do what?

C – General First Aid – 10 Points

1 How and where do you apply a tourniquet?
2 Give the treatment for fainting.
3 Give the treatment for sun-stroke.
4 Give the treatment for wounds.
5 Give the treatment for and symptoms of shock.

D – Wig-Wag – 10 points

Translate into code 'Go send them help quick.'
Translate into English '1121-12-3-1121-22-11-2-3-22-3-2112-21-22-2-333.'

E – Write an essay on general methods, precautions, etc., for rescuing. – 20 Points

F – Write an essay on how you would restore an apparently drowned man to consciousness. – 20 Points

G – Practical First Aid (Make appointment with the doctor.)

General hints

Kick!
If you work your hands like paddles and kick your feet, you can stay above water for several hours, even with your clothes on. It requires a little courage and enough strength of mind not to lose your head.

Cramps
Many boy swimmers make the mistake of going into the water too soon after eating. The stomach and digestive organs are busy preparing the food for the blood and body. Suddenly they are called upon to care for the work of the swimmer. The change is too quick for the organs, the process of digestion stops. Congestion is apt to follow, and then the paralysing cramps.

Indian Method

The Indians have a method of protecting themselves from cramps. Coming to a bathing pool, an Indian swimmer, after stripping off and before entering the water, vigorously rubs the pit of his stomach with the dry palms of his hands. This rubbing probably takes a minute; then he dashes cold water all over his stomach and continues the rubbing for another minute, and after that he is ready for his plunge. If the water in which you are going to swim is cold, try this Indian method of getting ready before plunging into the water.

Rule

The rule for entering the water, in most camps, is as follows: 'No one of the party shall enter the water for swimming or bathing except at time and place designated.' Laxity in the observance of this rule will result disastrously.

Rescue from drowning

Rescue

To rescue a drowning person from the water, always try to pull him out with an oar, a rope, a coat (holding the end of one sleeve and throwing him the other), or some other convenient object. If you are obliged to jump in after him, approach him with great caution, throw your left arm around his neck with his back to your side, in which position he can't grapple you, and swim with your legs and right arm. If he should succeed in grasping you, take a long breath, sink with him, place your feet or knees against his body, and push yourself free.

Although life may seem extinct, make every effort at resuscitation. Various procedures are advocated. The Sylvester method is one of the best.

Tear off clothing. Rub briskly the legs and arms toward the body. Draw the tongue forward every three seconds for a minute. If these methods fail to restore breathing, then perform artificial respiration, first sending for a physician.

Lay the boy on his back with a folded coat or sweater under his shoulders, and grasp his wrists or his arms straight up over his head.

Pull steadily and firmly in that position while you count 1, 2, 3. This causes air to enter the lungs. Then quickly bring his arms down on his chest and press them firmly on his ribs while you again count 1, 2, 3. This forces the air out of the lungs. Then quickly carry his arms over his head and down again, and repeat the same routine fast enough to make him breathe from twelve to sixteen times a minute. The tendency is to work too fast. If the work is done properly the air can be heard distinctly as it passes in and out of the air passages. Sometimes the tongue drops back in the throat, stopping it up so no air can enter. If you suspect this, have an assistant grasp the tongue with a handkerchief and keep it pulled forward.

Don't Give Up

It will make it much easier if you have another person push on the ribs for you when you relax the arms. Have him place the hands with the thumbs toward the medium line in front, the fingers farther away, the palms just below the breasts; this will make the boy's nipples come just midway between the ends of the thumbs and the middle joint of the forefinger. Press firmly downward and inward toward the backbone.

Continue these motions about fifteen times per minute. Keep this up until the boy begins to breathe, himself. When done properly, the work is hard for the operator, and he should be relieved by some one else as soon as he gets tired.

Warmth and Quiet

As soon as the boy begins to breathe himself — but not before — his limbs should be well rubbed toward the heart. This will help to restore the circulation. He should afterward be put to bed, well covered with warm blankets, hot stones being placed at his feet, and warm drinks administered. Fresh air and quiet will do the rest.

Books

Boys' Drill Regulation, published by the National First Aid Association of America, and *Boys' Life Brigade Manual of Drill*, published by the Boys' Life Brigade, London, England, are two small books containing a number of practical drills which may be used in training the boys in camp for emergency work.

Instruction

Every camp for boys, no matter how small or how large, should plan for instruction in First Aid. This may be done by the camp physician, the director, the physical director, or some physician invited to spend several days in the camp.

Drills

The 'litter' drill was especially attractive to the boys of one camp. The boys were sent out in the woods in brigades of five each, one of whom was the leader. Only a small hatchet was taken by each squad. One of the boys was supposed to have broken his leg. An improvised 'litter,' or, stretcher, was made of saplings or boughs, strapped together with handkerchiefs and belts, so that in ten minutes after they left the camp the first squad returned with the boy on the litter and in a fairly comfortable condition.

Health Talks

A course of health talks given in popular form by those who are well versed upon the subject, cannot help but be instructive and productive of a greater ambition on the part of the boy to take good care of his body. The following list of subjects is suggestive:

The Human Body and How to Keep It in Health

1   The Skeleton.
2   The Muscular System.
3   The Vascular System.
4   The Nervous System.
5   The Digestive System.
6   The Lungs, Skin and Kidneys.

Personal Hygiene

1   The Eye, its use and abuse.
2   How to care for the Teeth.
3   Breathing and pure air.
4   Microbes and keeping clean.
7   The health of the Skin.
8   Some facts about the Nose.
9   Our Lungs.
10 Eating.
11 Alcohol.
12 Tobacco and the Human Body.
13 The Use and Care of Finger Nails.
14 Cause of Colds.

Honour points are given boys for essays written upon the Health Talks. Some camps found that boys were desirous of taking examinations in First Aid.

16

Personal Hygiene

Eating

Very little thought is given by the boy to what he eats, as long as it suits his taste, and there is an ample supply. The causes of most skin diseases are largely traceable to diet. Chew the food slowly. Don't 'bolt' food. Your stomach is not like that of a dog. Food must be thoroughly masticated and moistened with saliva. Hasty chewing and swallowing of food makes masses which tend to sour and become poison. This often accounts for the belching of gas, sense of burning and pain, and other forms of distress after eating. Drink before or after meals. Don't overeat. Conversation aids digestion. Eating between meals is detrimental to good digestion. Regular meal hours should prevail. After dinner is the best time to eat candy or sweets.

The Teeth

If the tooth brush gets lost make one out of a dry stick, about six inches long, which can be frayed out at the ends like the illustration, opposite. A clean mouth is as important as a clean body. The teeth should be cleaned twice a day, morning and evening. Insist upon the bringing of a tooth brush to camp. Impress upon the boys that time spent upon teeth cleansing will prevent hours of agony upon a dentist chair. Cleansing the teeth of sticky deposits by running fine threads between them, in addition to the use of a brush and a simple powder, prevents deposits from becoming the starting point of decay.

The Hands

Care of hands and nails is much neglected in camp, Nails should be properly trimmed and the 'mourning' removed from underneath the nails. The habit of biting the finger nails is dangerous. Finger nails should be cut once a week with sharp scissors or 'clip.' If the nails be neglected and a scratch received from the infected fingers the system may be inoculated with disease. The cleansing of the hands after using the lavatory needs special emphasis, for in no place do more germs collect and spread. Boys should not be permitted to use each

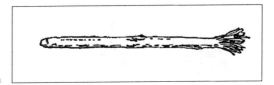

Camp tooth brush

other's towels, combs, brushes, or soap. A towel may carry germs from one boy to another.

The Eyes

Never strain the eyes. When reading, always let the light come over the shoulder and upon the page, the eyes being in the shadow. Do not read with the sunlight streaming across the page. When writing have the light come from the left side. Do not rub the eyes with the hands. Headaches and nervousness are due largely to defective vision. 'Work, play, rest and sleep, muscular exercise, wise feeding, and regular removal of the waste – these and all other hygienic habits help to keep the eyes sound and strong.' (Sedgewick)

The Ear

It is dangerous to put a pointed pencil or anything sharpened into the ear. 'Boxing' the ear, shouting in the ear, exploding a paper bag, may split the drum and cause deafness. The best way to remove excess wax from the ear is to use a soft, damp cloth over the end of the finger. Ear-wax is a protection against insects getting in from the outside.

The Nose

Keep the nose free from obstructions, and avoid the use of dirty handkerchiefs. Always breathe through the nose and not through the mouth. Boys who observe this rule will not get thirsty while on a hike or get out of breath so easily. They don't breathe in all sorts of microbes or seeds of disease, and they don't snore at night.

The Hair

In washing the hair avoid using soap more than once a week, as it removes the natural oil of the hair. Frequent combing and brushing adds to the lustre, and the head gets a beneficial form of massage. Wear no hat at camp, except to protect from sun rays or rain.

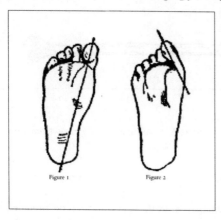

Figure 1   Figure 2

The Feet

Footwear is a matter of importance. Shoes should never be worn too tight. They not only hinder free movements, but also hinder the blood circulation, and cause coldness and numbness of the extremities. Sore feet, because of ill-fitting shoes, are a detriment to happy camp life. Have good, well-fitting, roomy shoes, and fairly stout ones. Keep the feet dry. If they are allowed to get wet, the skin is softened and very soon gets blistered and rubbed raw.

The figure on the left shows a perfectly shaped foot. This is the natural shape, and if the boy is allowed to go barefooted or wear sandals, his foot will assume this shape. The figure on the right shows the distorted shape brought about by cramped shoes. The best thing to wear is thick moccasins of moose hide.

Internal Organs

Constipation is a frequent camp complaint, and is usually the result of change in diet and drinking water. The habit of having a daily movement of the bowels is of great importance to a boy's health. The retention of these waste products within the body for a longer period tends to produce poisonous impurities of the blood, a muddy-looking skin, headaches, piles, and many other evils. Eat plenty of fruit, prunes, and graham bread. Drink plenty of water. Take plenty of exercise.

Bathing

One bath a day in fresh water is all that is necessary. Boys go into the water too often and remain too long. This accounts for the rundown appearance of some boys. The body gives off heat every minute it is in cool water, and also when exposed wet to the breezes, and heat is life. All boys should be encouraged to take a dip before breakfast with a rapid rubdown. Then a good swim in the warm part of the day. Usually about 11:30 a.m. is a good time for the swim. If a swim is taken after supper, be careful to dress warm afterward.

Sleep

Normal boys need nine or ten hours sleep. Sleep is a time for physical growth. Have the tent open back and front at night to insure plenty of fresh air. There must be a complete change of clothing on retiring. Flannel clothing should be worn at night. Sleep alone. Nine o'clock or nine-thirty, at latest, should find every boy in bed.

Clothing

Wear clean clothing, particularly underwear. Frequently a rash appearing on the body is a result of wearing dirty-shirts. The wearing of belts tends to constrict the abdomen, thus hindering the natural action of the intestines, which is essential to good digestion. Hernia (ruptures) may result from wearing tightly drawn belts. To dress the body too warm lessens the power to resist cold when there happens to be a change in the atmosphere. Put on extra clothing at sundown, without waiting to begin to feel cold. During eating of meals it is well to have the legs and arms covered when it is at all cool. The cooling of large surfaces of the body while eating, even if it is not noticed, retards digestion, and taxes the vitality. Many a boy gets a cold by neglecting to take this precaution.

General Hints

Two flannel shirts are better than two overcoats.

Don't wring out flannels or woollens. Wash in cold water, very soapy, and then hang them up dripping wet, and they will not shrink.

If you keep your head from getting hot, and keep your feet dry, there will be little danger of sickness.

If your head gets too hot, put green leaves inside your hat.

If your throat is parched and you can get no water, put a pebble in your mouth. This will start the saliva and quench the thirst.

Health Maxims and Quotations

Keep thyself pure.

Health is wealth.

A sound mind in a sound body.

Fresh air and sunshine are necessary to good health.

Cleanliness is the best guard against disease.

A clean mouth is as important as a clean body.

Virtue never dwelt long with filth.

Temperance, exercise, and repose
Slam the door on the doctor's nose.
>> (Longfellow)

Cleanliness is next to Godliness.

Health and cheerfulness naturally beget each other.
>> (Addison)

Nor love, nor honor, wealth nor power,
Can give the heart a cheerful hour,
When health is lost. Be truly wise.
With health, all taste of pleasure flies.
>> (Gay)

Health is a second blessing that we mortals are capable of: a blessing that money cannot buy.

>> (Walton)

There are three wicks, you know, to the lamp of a man's life: brain, blood, and breath. Press the brain a little, its light goes out, followed by both the others. Stop the heart a minute, and out go all three of the wicks. Choke the air out of the lungs, and presently the fluid ceases to supply the other centres of flame, and all is soon stagnation, cold, and darkness.

>> (O.W. Holmes)

17

Athletics, Campus Games, Aquatics and Water Sports

If I can teach these boys to study and play together, freely and with fairness to one another, I shall make them fit to live and work together in society.

(Henry van Dyke)

Purpose of Games

The spirit of camping is too frequently destroyed by over-emphasis upon competitive games. Play is necessary for the growing boy and play that engages many participants has the most value. Today we are suffering from highly specialised, semi-professional athletics and games.

> When athletics degenerate into a mere spectacle, then is the stability of the nation weakened. Greece led the world, while the youth of that great country deemed it an honour to struggle for the laurel leaf, and gymnasiums were everywhere and universally used and the people saw little good in an education that neglected the body. It is a significant fact that the degeneracy of Greece was synchronous with the degrading of athletics into mere professional contests. What had been the athletics of the people became a spectacle for the people.[1]

Cricket

Do not allow the athletics and games of the camp to become a mere spectacle for the campers. Something should be planned for every boy and every boy encouraged to participate in the programme. Nothing has yet taken the place of the good old English game of cricket. Divide the camp boys into teams. Have a league playing a series of games. The teams may be named after prominent cities or as one camp named the league, the 'Food League' after popular camp dishes, such as: 'Prunes', 'Beans', 'Soup', 'Hash', 'Mush', 'Chipped Beef'. It is needless to state that the boys in the league not only had a lot of fun, but the camp paper contained very amusing accounts of the games played.

Arrange a schedule of games and keep accurate records of all games played either in the 'Camp Log' or camp paper. A dinner given to the winning team adds to the excitement of the league's existence. Do not neglect the younger boys; have two younger teams engage in a series for best two out of three games. Occasionally a game between the leaders and older boys is the exciting game of the season, especially if the leaders are defeated.

The same rule of participation should govern the athletics of the camp. Inter-tent games help to develop group loyalty, cooperation, fair play, and courtesy to opponents so desirable.

Groups

In some camps the boys are divided into two groups, those under five feet in height and those over five feet. Events are planned for these two groups. The system of grouping suggested by the School Athletic League, is that of grouping the boys according to physiological rather than chronological age, as follows:

Pre-pubescent boys under 90 pounds.

Pubescent boys or juniors, 90 to 110 pounds.

Post-pubescent or intermediates, 110 to 130 pounds.

Seniors, above 130 pounds.

The boys are weighed in competing costume. This system is looked upon as being fair and practical.

What to Avoid

The following should be avoided – Marathon runs, sustained effort in and under water and competitive long-distance running. The longest sprint race should be, for boys, 50 yards, for juniors, 75 yards. No adolescent who is not past the pubescent stage should run sprint races longer than 100 yards. Cross-country running is beneficial when taken at a slow pace and without competition. Every boy should be examined for heart weakness before enter-ing the strenuous games.

Events

The athletics usually planned for camp are: 50 yard dash for boys; 75-yard dash for juniors; 100 yard dash for seniors; running high jump; running broad jump; pole vault; 8 and 12-pound shot-put and relay race.

Awards

Ribbon awards presented to the winners at a special meeting of the campers aid considerably in fostering the true spirit of clean athletics and wholesome sport

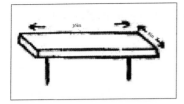

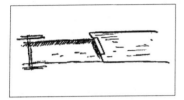

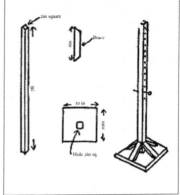

Top left: Take-off

Above left: Cross-section of take-off

Above right: Jumping standards

and are appreciated by the winners as souvenirs of the good-natured contest.

A perpetual cup for all-round proficiency, upon which is engraved the name of each year's winner, is a good way of recording the annual athletic meet.

A shield with the names of the winners of the season's events painted or burned upon it and hung up in the camp lodge helps to retain the interest of the winner in the camp after he has become a 'grown-up' or alumnus.

Apparatus

Boys who like to make things may be put to work making various pieces of athletic apparatus. A take-off may be made of a plank or board, 8 inches wide and 36 inches long, sunk flush with the earth. The outer edge of this plank is considered the scratch line. Remove the earth to a depth of three inches and width of twelve inches.

To make a pair of jumping standards, first saw out the bottom blocks, each being 10 x 10 inches and 2 inches thick. In the centre of each block chisel out a hole 2 x 2 inches and about 1 inch in depth. Into these holes fit the ends of the upright pieces, which should be 5 feet long and 2 inches square. Before securing the upright pieces, bore holes an inch apart, into which may be inserted a piece of heavy wire or large wire nail to hold up the cross piece or jumping stick. Be sure to space the holes alike on both uprights, so the crosspiece will set level when the standard is in use. Four 5-inch braces are fastened in at the lower part of the upright. Study the diagram and you will succeed in making a pretty good pair of standards.

Campus Games

After supper is usually a period in the camp life rather difficult of occupation. 'Campus Games' appeal to most boys. These games are designed especially for the after-supper hour, although they may be played at any time.

Circle Jumping

Stand the boys in a circle with all hands clasped. One of the crowd lies down in the centre with a rope as long as one-half the diameter of the circle. To the end of the rope is tied a small weight like a sand bag. He whirls the weight around with the full length of rope revolving with increasing rapidity. As it approaches the players, they hop up and let it pass under their feet. The one whose foot is touched is out of the game and the boy who keeps out of the way of the rope the longest is the winner.

Wolf

Here is a Japanese game full of fun and action. Place a dozen or more boys in line, and have each fellow place his hands firmly on the shoulders of the boy in front of him. Choose one of the fellows for the 'Wolf'. The first boy at the head of the line is called the 'Head' of the Serpent, and the last fellow is the 'Tail'. The 'Wolf' stands near the head of the Serpent until a signal is given. Then he tries to catch the 'Tail' without touching any other part of the snake. The boys who form the body of the Serpent protect the 'Tail' by wreathing about in all sorts of twists to prevent the 'Wolf' from catching the 'Tail'. This must be done without breaking the line. When the 'Tail' is caught, the 'Wolf' becomes the 'Head,' and the 'Tail' becomes the 'Wolf.' The last boy in line is the 'Tail'. The game can be continued until every boy has been the 'Wolf'.

Rover, All Come Over

A line is marked dividing the campus. All the boys gather on one side. One boy in the centre endeavours to have them step over the line by calling out, 'Rover, Rover, all come over!' At the word 'over' everybody is expected to run and cross the line, while the centre man endeavours to catch one. The one caught must help him catch the others. If any one runs over before the centre man calls 'over', he has to go to the aid of the catcher. When all are caught the game begins again.

Indian and White Man

The game of 'Indian and White Man' is interesting. A circle is drawn on the campus. It is supposed that the white people are travelling over the prairie, and at night time they prepare to camp. The circle represents their camp. The Whites lie down to sleep and sentries are posted. The Indians discover the camp and endeavour to capture the Whites. Then comes the battle royal. Every Indian captured in the white man's circle counts one, and every white man captured by the Indians outside the circle counts one for their side. The game continues until all of either side are captured. The players are divided into two groups. The Indians are concealed in the bushes or some place unseen by the Whites and they make the attack.

Such games as 'Three Deep', 'Bull in the Ring', 'Tag Game', 'Leap Frog', will be found to interest the boys during the after-supper period.

The following are campus games requiring apparatus:

German Bowling

Plant in the ground two posts, leaving at least 15 feet above ground. Spike a 10-foot piece across the top. An ordinary ball used in bowling is used by plugging shut the holes and inserting a screw eye in one of the plugged holes. Tie tightly to this screw eye a strong piece of rope. A good-sized screw eye is fastened in the cross piece of the frame, and to this tie the ball. Nine bowling pins are used. The score is the same as bowling. The pins are knocked off by the return of the ball, as shown in the diagram.

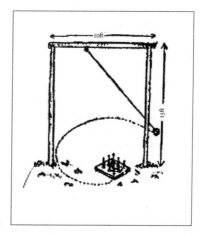

German bowling

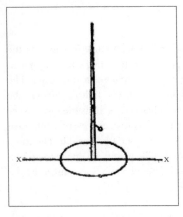

Tether ball

Tether Ball

The upright pole should be standing ten feet out of the ground and firmly imbedded in the earth so as not to vibrate.

The pole should be 7-1/2 inches in circumference at the ground and tapering toward the upper end. Paint a black or white 2-inch band around the pole 6 feet above the ground. Draw a circle about the pole on the ground having a 3-foot radius. A 20-foot line must bisect the circle. Use a tennis ball having a netted or tightly fitting linen cover. The ball is fastened to a string with a ring and suspended from the top of the pole by a piece of heavy braided fish line. The cord should allow the ball to hang 7-1/2 feet. Tennis racquets are used. The two players stand at point marked with an X in the diagram. In the toss-up for courts the loser is the server. The ball may be struck in any manner with the racquet, the endeavour being to wind the string upon the pole above the painted band.

Volley Ball

Stretch a tennis net across the campus and mark a court fifty feet long, to be divided equally by the net. The play consists in keeping in motion the ball over the net from one side to the other, until one fails to return it, which counts as an out. The ball used is similar to a football, only smaller. The game consists of twenty-one points.

Many of the camps have tennis courts and hold tournaments. This game is so universal and familiar that no description will be made.

Aquatic Sports and Water Games

Aquatic sports may be arranged so that active interest will be taken by all the boys, or they may be simply an exhibition of the swimming abilities of several boys. The former is decidedly preferable. Events should be arranged for the small as well as the large boys.

The programme of events should include a short dash, swimming under water, diving for form, fancy swimming and special stunts, ribbon awards or inexpensive cups to be given the winners. The Life Saving Corps will have an opportunity to give an exhibition of their skill and alertness, as well as patrol the swimming beach. Good reliable fellows should be appointed to watch each swimmer when in the water. Run no chances at any time that boys are in the water. The following water games have been suggested by A.B. Wegener:

1 Three-legged swimming.
2 Tug of War.
3 Bobbing for Corks.
4 Plunging through hoops for height or distance.
5 Diving for objects.
6 Egg Race; holding the egg in a spoon either in the mouth or hand.
7 Tag games.
8 Potato race; using corks instead of potatoes.
9 Candle race; candles are lighted and must be kept lighted.
10 Various land games may be adapted for water use, such as ball passing (using a water polo ball), relay race, etc.

Water Basketball

Two peach baskets, or rope baskets, or two iron rings are hung upon poles five feet above the water and forty feet apart. The game is played similarly to basketball, except that the players are allowed to advance with the ball. Tackling and ducking are fouls and penalised by allowing a free throw for goal from a point fifteen feet away.

There is no out of bounds, and a basket may be thrown from any place in the water. A field goal counts two points, and a goal from a foul one point.

Water Baseball

The outfit required is a tennis ball, a broom stick and four rafts – one large and three small. The batsman and catcher stand on the big raft. On a small raft, ten yards away, stands the pitcher and the other two rafts are placed at easy swimming distance for bases. In striking, everything counts – bunt, swat or foul tip. The moment bat and ball come in contact the batsman starts for first base. There are five men on a side. Lots of fun. Avoid remaining in fresh water too long as it has a tendency to weaken vitality.

Old Clothes Race

The contestants are dressed in a full suit of old clothes. At the word 'go' they dive into the water and swim to a float placed at a certain distance away, undress and return. This is a very funny race.

Tilting

Two boats manned by four boys each. One boy is the spearman and is armed with a light pole about eight or ten feet long, having a soft pad of rags, or better yet, of water-proof canvas duck to keep it from getting wet and soggy. If a flat-bottom boat is used, the spearman stands on one of the end seats. A quarter-deck or raised platform should be built on an ordinary boat or canoe. The battle is fought in rounds and by points. If you put your opponent back into the boat with one foot it counts you 5; two feet, 10. If he loses his spear you count 5 (except when he is put overboard). If you put him down on one knee on the 'fighting deck,' you count 5; two knees, 10. If you put him overboard it counts 25. One hundred points is a round. A battle is for one or more rounds as agreed upon. It is forbidden to strike below the belt. The umpire may dock for fouls.

Canoe Tag

Any number of canoes or boats may engage in this water game. A rubber football is used. The game is to tag the other canoe or boat by throwing this into it. The rules are as in ordinary cross tag.

Whale Hunt

The 'whale' is made of a big log of wood with a rough-shaped head and tail to represent a whale. Two boats are used, each manned by the boys of one tent – the leader acting as captain, a boy as bowman or harpooner, the others as oarsmen. Each boat belongs to a different harbour, the two harbours being some distance apart. The umpire takes the 'whale' and lets it loose about half-way between the two harbours and on a signal the two boats race out to see who can get to the 'whale' first. The harpooner who first arrives within range of the 'whale' drives his harpoon into it and the boat promptly turns around and tows the 'whale' to its harbour. The second boat pursues and when it overtakes the other, also harpoons the 'whale', turns around and endeavours to tow the 'whale' to its harbour. In this way the two boats have a tug-of-war and eventually the better boat tows the 'whale' and possibly the opposing boat into its harbour.

Shoot-the-Chute

A 'Shoot-the-Chute' is great fun and one should be built in every permanent camp and 'Swimming Hole.' The one described is by A.D. Murray and has stood the test of several years in a number of camps.

The plan drawn is for a chute 40 feet long, 3 feet wide and 18 feet high. These dimensions can be changed in length and height, but not in width. The chute is built of 7/8 inch matched pine boards, to the same width as sheet zinc, usually 3 feet; the boards being firmly cleated together on the under side by 2 x 6 inch cleats 5 feet apart, throughout the length of the chute. Boards should be screwed to the cleats from the face of the chute with 1-1/2 inch screws, the heads being counter sunk. The several lengths of zinc are soldered into one piece, the joints being on the under side (as shingles on a roof) fastened to the boards with 8-oz. tacks; set in from the edge about 1 inch and about 6 inches apart. The side strips of maple (soft wood will not do on account of the danger of splintering) 2 inches wide and 3 inches high, rounded slightly on upper edge, are placed directly over the edge of the zinc and covering the tacks. Screw the strips firmly to the chute with 2 inch screws from the under side. These ought to be placed not more than 2 feet apart. Probably each will have two or more strips in making a piece of sufficient length. If so, care should be taken to have the pieces joined on a bevel with a slant from outer edge

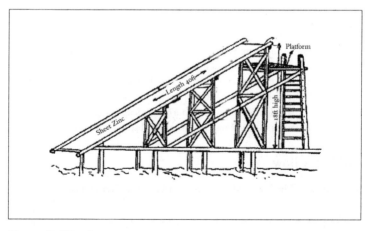

Diagram for 'Chute'

toward bottom of chute so as to leave no edge. The utmost care should be used to have a perfectly smooth surface on the inside of the chute. A pump or bucket is needed at the top of the chute to wet the surface before the swimmer starts his slide. The supports A, B, C, should be firmly braced with 2 x 4 inch timber, D, and lower end of chute should extend over the pier at least 1 foot and not nearer the surface of the water than 3 feet perpendicularly, allowing the swimmer to enter the water as in a dive. The chute can be fastened to the supporting braces through timbers E, F, into maple side strips with a good heavy log screw. A platform 3 feet wide and 4 feet long near the top of chute, and set just waist deep from the top of chute will make starting easy.

Archery

Richard the Lion-hearted, of England, said the five essential points of archery – standing, nocking,[2] drawing, holding, and loosing – 'honestly represented all the principles of life.'

Archery develops the muscles in all-round fashion, particularly those of the shoulder, arm and wrist.

The Target

A target can be made of a burlap sack, or oil cloth, about five feet square. Stuff this with hay or straw. It may be flattened by a few quilting stitches put right through with a long packing needle. On this the target is painted. In scoring, the centre is 9, the next circle 7, the next 5, the next 3 and the last circle 1. The shortest match range for the target is forty yards.

The Bow

The bow may be made from any of the following woods – mulberry, sassafras, southern cedar, black locust, black walnut, apple, slippery elm or hickory. In making a bow, select wood with straight grain. The length of the bow should be about the height of the boy using it, or if the boy is between ten and fifteen years of age, his bow should not be less than four feet in length and not more than five feet. When buying a bow get one of lancewood backed with hickory.

Making A Bow

The making of the bow and arrow is described by A. Neeley Hall, as follows:

> Cut your piece of wood five feet long, and, after placing it in a bench vice to hold it in position, shape it down with a drawknife or plane until it is

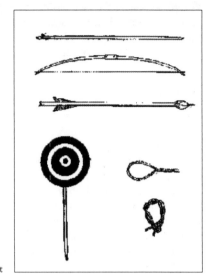

Notch for bowstrings; length of bow 5 feet. Wire nail with head cut off (arrow head). Old canvas stuffed (target); loop (in bowstring); slip knot

one inch wide by one-half inch thick at the handle, and three quarters inch wide by one-quarter inch thick at the ends. The bow can be made round or flat on the face toward the archer. Cut a notch in the bow two inches from each end, as shown in the illustration, from which to attach the bow-string. A cord with as little elasticity as possible should be used for this.

With a home-made bow-string, a loop should be made in one end and bound with thread, as shown in the illustration above. Slip the loop over the upper notch, bend the bow until the center of the string is about five inches away from the handle, and attach the loose end to the lower notch by means of a slip-knot similar to that shown in the drawing. The bow should then be sandpapered until smooth, and thoroughly oiled with linseed oil. Glue a piece of velvet about three inches wide around the center for a handle.

Making Arrows

Arrows are divided into three parts: the head, sometimes called the pile, the shaft and the feathers. The shaft is generally made of hickory, ash, elm or pine, and its length is dependent upon that of the bow. For a five-foot bow, make the length two feet and the width and thickness about one-half inch. For target practice a wire nail driven into the end of the pile, as shown above, with the head of the nail filed off and pointed, makes an excellent head. Feathering is the next operation. Turkey and goose feathers are generally used. Strip off the broader side of the vane of three feathers and glue them to the shaft one inch and a quarter from the notch, spacing them equally from each other. One feather should be placed at right angles to the notch. This is known as the cock feather and should always point away from the bow when the arrow is shot.

Archery

The rules for the five essential points are these:

Standing: In taking position to draw the bow, the heels must be seven to eight inches apart, feet firm on the ground, yet easy and springy, not rigid.

Nocking: This is manipulating the bow string. Hold the string with two fingers and the arrow between the first and second fingers. Grip firmly, but not so as to give awkwardness to any finger.

Drawing: In drawing stand with the left shoulder toward the target, turning the head only from the neck and looking over the left shoulder. Then raise the bow with the left hand, keeping the upper end inclined one or two degrees from the body. With the right hand draw the arrow to chin-level and below the ear.

Holding: Steady the aim a moment and keep the point of aim directly in view, looking along the whole length of the arrow.

Loosing: In letting the arrow go, do not jerk, but loose smoothly, and be certain your bow arm does not move when loosing. To get a clean, sharp loose is more than half way to hitting the target.

Bibliography

Indoor and Outdoor Game. (188) – A. M. Chesley. American Sports Publishing Co.

An Athletic Primer, Group XII., No.87 – J.E. Sullivan. American Sports Publishing Co.

Official Handbook Y.M.C.A. Athletic League, Group XII., No.302. – American Sports Publishing Co. Tether Tennis, Volley Ball, Etc., No.188. – American Sports Publishing Co.

At Home in the Water – George H. Corsan. Association Press. Twenty pages of this excellent book are devoted to water sports, and it also contains complete rules for Water Polo, a splendid game for adults, but unwise to play in a boys' camp.

The Birch Bark Roll – Ernest Thompson-Seton. Doubleday, Page & Co.

Two Little Savages – Ernest Thompson-Seton. Doubleday, Page & Co.

These books give valuable hints on Archery, which is peculiarly adapted for camp life and sport.

The Witchery of Archery – Maurice Thompson. Charles Scribner's Sons. Fascinating and entertaining.

18

Nature Study

If nature is to be a resource in a man's life, one's relation to her must not be too exact and formal, but more that of a lover and friend.

(John Burroughs)

Outdoor Instinct

'The boy is always nearer to the heart of nature than the grown man. He has a passionate love of the open air and of the fields and woods; he is never really happy indoors. Nature has planted this outdoor instinct in the boy's heart for the good of the race.' Day and night teach him their lessons. The boy will absorb much that is interesting and also much that will be of real value in giving him a broader outlook upon life. Camping gives abundant opportunity for the study of nature.

Nature study is not a fad of modern times. Nearly three hundred and fifty years before Christ, Alexander the Great placed at the disposal of his tutor, Aristotle, the services of one thousand men throughout Asia and Greece with instructions to collect and report details concerning the life, conditions and habits of fishes, birds, beasts and insects.

Prof. L.H. Bailey says,

The modern idea of Nature Study is, to put the boy in a sympathetic attitude toward nature for the purpose of increasing the joy of living. Nature study is not science. It is not knowledge. It is spirit. It is concerned with the boy's outlook on the world ... This Nature spirit is growing, and there are many ways of knowing the fields and woods. A new literature has been born. It is the literature of the out-of-doors.

Collectors

Boys are natural born collectors. They are interrogation points, full of curiosity, like the 'man from Missouri,' they want to know. The wise leader will say, 'Let us find out some thing about this tree, or plant, or bird, or whatever it may be, and together we will be learners.' The textbook method will not work in a boys' camp. 'Go find me a flower' is the true method, and let us see what it is. Nature study books and leaflets should be used merely as guides, not as texts.

Arousing Interest

Arouse interest by encouraging the boys to make collections of leaves, flowers, etc., found in the vicinity of the camp. Leaves and flowers may be pressed in a home-made press and mounted upon heavy paper or cardboard. The following suggestions are given by Dan Beard and quoted by permission of Charles Scribner's Sons from his Book, *The Field and Forest Handy Book*.

Herbarium

The illustration below shows how the press is made. In using the press, first place the plants or leaves, enclosed in their wrappers and dryers of newspapers, on the bottom board, put the top board over them, bring the hinged lever down and bind the whole together with a stout strap put around the end of the lever and the handle of the bottom board. As this strap is drawn tight the lever bends, and so keeps a constant pressure on the plants and leaves even when they shrink in drying. Dryers should be changed at least every day. Mount specimens on separate herbarium sheets of standard size (1-1/2 x 16-1/2). Each specimen should be mounted with name (common and botanical), where found, date and any other facts of interest. This label is usually pasted in the lower right hand corner of the herbarium sheet.

Equipment

If the camp has a permanent building, these specimens make a most attractive decoration as well as help to recall the happy days of 'the hunt.' The material equipment for nature study should consist of a good loose leaf note-book,

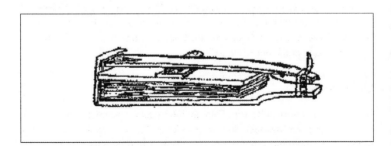

The Vreeland press

something that will stand the out-door wear. Get quadrille ruled sheets. They will simplify sketching in the matter of proportion and scale. A pocket magnifying glass will serve for identification of the specimens. Best of all is a high-power microscope, especially where the camp has a permanent building with suitable room, having a good light and table facilities. A camera will help in securing permanent records of trees, ferns, flowers, birds, freaks of nature and scenes other than the usual camp groups. A few reliable books on nature study are needed to complete the outfit.

Hunting

A 'bird hunt' was a popular sport in one of my camps. We started off early one morning, a group of boys, each 'loaded' with a big lunchbox crammed with good things, a note-book, a book on bird-life, and a 'gun.' The 'gun' we used was a powerful pair of field glasses. On the way we counted the number of bird-homes we saw. Just as we were thinking about stopping and having breakfast we heard a most ecstatic song. Creeping close to the place where the sound came from, we discovered the songster to be a song-sparrow. Focussing our 'gun' upon the bird we made note of its colouring and marking, making sure that if we heard or saw another we would recognise it at once. While we were eating our breakfast, there was a dash of white, yellow, and greyish-brown, a whirring sound and, as the bird lighted upon the low bushes near-by, a clear, piercing whistle came from its throat. Our 'gun' revealed to us a meadow lark. By this time the boys were as much excited over the bird hunt as over a game of ball.

Walks Afield

A 'flower walk,' observing the wild flowers; a 'fern walk,' discerning the delicate tracery of the fern in its cool haunts; a 'tree walk', noting the different trees – all are natural ways of interesting boys in nature study.

Night Sounds

G.B. Affleck in the April 1910 number of Physical Training tells his experience in studying nature with several groups of boys:

The night sounds surrounding a camp in northern Minnesota were a puzzle to boys and to the counsellor of the tent at the end of the row. This problem continued unsolved for more than a week, despite all attempts both by day and night. Finally, one moist, warm night, Ned, after stealthily approaching the sound, satisfied himself of its location in a certain tree and in the morning was rewarded by the discovery of the 'toad' camped on a branch near the source whence the sound had issued. Replacing the frog so that the coarse tubercles of its back corresponded to the bark, Ned enjoyed a merited reward at the expense of his tent mates who, though often 'hot,' required some minutes to find the hidden treasure. Then came the wonder of the stick toes and fingers, the feeding with flies, and the result was – a new pet for the tent. In the next letters written to the folks this find was the central theme. How much better this discovery and the examination of the peculiar colors and structures, also the conclusions, based upon observed structure, as to the life and habits of the tree frog than would have been a scientifically learned discussion of the family Hylidae!

In a camp of fifty boys the writer remembers three who had special delight in collecting pebbles, and they made several all-day trips to distant brooks and beaches in the search for new specimens. Another group became so fascinated with the study of the food of fish that they begged the 'privilege' of cleaning the catch of each returning party. Proud was that lad who incidentally located the heart of a pickerel, and because of his school knowledge of physiology he could not be convinced that the fish breathed without lungs till he had spent many hours in the vain endeavour to locate said organs. Then he knew that his former idea had been inadequate.

Fishology

Fortunately, nature is so interrelated in her various phases that an attempt at exploration in one direction soon opens other fields, until with the growth of experience there comes a corresponding expansion of interest. Thus the lads, searching for pebbles, were perforce attracted by the plant and insect life of the brook, and the one delving into the mystery of breathing oxygen without lungs developed a new interest in the physics of fluids, while those who located the tree frog enlarged their sphere by the knowledge that their pet rejected some of the 'bugs' offered it.

The leader, commencing thus with the limited or special interest of each group, may evolve in his own mind the plan which most naturally will lead the boys not only into a wider field of concrete facts, but also into the habit of seeing relationships, of drawing conclusions and of raising questions for further investigation.

A group of boys interested in a study of fish may well be organised for an all-day trip to the root of the rapids or the bay of springs; others with geological preferences may spend a night on the top of the distant hill which offers outcroppings of interest; the embryo botanists cannot do better than to take a bog trot for the rare orchid, anomalous pitcher plant, or glistening sun dew; lovers of the deep shade may paddle to the inlet of the creek and there enjoy a side trip on the fragrant carpet of hemlock and pine needles; thus it will be found that by anticipating the probable findings in which the particular group is interested the leader gives a point and purpose, adding not only to the enjoyment of the outing, but imparting, in addition, some satisfactory knowledge of the vicinity.

Longfellow said that a 'strong evidence of goodly character was the thoughtful-ness one displayed in caring for a tree.' One of the best things at one camp was a series of out-door talks on nature given by Silas H. Berry. Seated on a huge rock, he told the boys about the shaping and clothing of the earth, foundation stones, mountains and hills, lakes, ponds, and rivers, the beginning of vegetable life, the variation and place of the freak, the forest and its place in the world's progress, the alternation of the forest crop, man and his neighbours. Another afternoon the boys went into the woods and while they squatted on Nature's mattress of fragrant pine needles, he told about leaves and their work, cells and their place, roots and their arrangement, tendrils and their mechanism, flowers and their devices, seeds and their travels. The third talk was upon the evolution of plant life, law and logic of creation, perpetuation of life in the lower forms, edible and poisonous mushrooms, and the perpetuation of life in the higher forms. The boys had a different conception of life thereafter and they possessed that nature-love which always tends toward naturalness and simplicity of living. They could sing with feeling.

> I love thy rocks and rills,
> Thy woods and templed hills.

Bibliography

How Nature Study Should be Taught – Edward F. Bigelow, Ph.D. Hinds, Noble and Eldridge. A book of inspiration. Many practical suggestions are given for arousing interest among boys in Nature Study.

The Nature Study Idea – Liberty H. Bailey. Macmillan Co. An interpretation of the new movement to put the boy in sympathy with Nature.

Field and Forest Handy Book – Dan Beard. Charles Scribner's Sons. Nothing better published for the benefit of those having permanent camps. It should be placed in the hands of every boy.

Outdoors, Indoors, and Up the Chimney – Charles McIlvaine. Sunday School Times Co. A series of interesting stories about commonplace things. Just the kind of information to give a boy on rainy days.

Dan Beard's Animal Book. Moffat, Yard & Company, $1.75 net. Filled with the kind of incidents about animals that boys delight to hear, including the famous bear stories. Also tells about the Campfire Club of Animals.

How to Study Birds – Herbert K. Job. Outing Publishing Co. Takes up the practical side of bird study. Describes the outfit necessary for studying the birds in the open. A valuable book.

Manual of Common American Insects – William Beautenmuller.

Manual of Common Butterflies and Moths – William Beautenmuller. Funk & Wagnalls Co. Two pocket manuals in which the insects, butterflies and moths are reproduced in natural colours with their common and scientific names.

Wilderness Pets at Camp Buckshaw – Edward Breck. Houghton, Mifflin Company. True tales of wilderness pets written by an experienced woodsman. Intensely interesting.

Young Folks' Nature Field Book – J. Alden Loring. Dana, Estes & Co. Contains a seasonable hint for every day in the year. The alternate pages are left blank for notes or record of things seen.

How to Know the Wild Flowers – F. T. Parsons. Charles Scribner's Sons.

How to Know the Ferns – F.T. Parsons. Charles Scribner's Sons.

Familiar Trees and Their Leaves – F.D. Matthews. Appleton and Company. Three reliable handbooks written in popular style.

An Out-of-Door Diary – Marion Miller. Sturgis and Walton Co. Suitable for very young boys.

19

Forecasting the Weather

Sunshine is delicious.
Rain is refreshing.
Wind braces up.
Snow is exhilarating.
There is really no such thing as bad weather,
only different kinds of good weather.

(Ruskin)

It is said that this weather table by Buzzacott is so near the truth as seldom or never to be found to fail.

Forecasting the Weather

If the New Moon, First Quarter, Full Moon, or Last Quarter,

comes between	In Summer	In Winter
12 and 2 a.m.	Fair	Frost, unless wind S.W.
2 and 4 a.m.	Cold and showers	Snow and stormy
4 and 6 a.m.	Rain	Rain
6 and 8 a.m.	Wind and rain	Stormy
8 and 10 a.m.	Changeable	Cold rain if wind W. Snow if E.
10 and 12 p.m.	Frequent showers	Cold and high wind
12 and 2 p.m.	Very rainy	Snow or rain
2 and 4 p.m.	Changeable	Fair and mild
4 and 6 .m.	Fair	Fair
6 and 8 p.m.	Fair if wind N.W.	Fair and frosty if wind N. or N.E.
8 and 10 p.m.	Rainy if S. or S.W.	Rain or snow if S. or S.W.
10 and 12 a.m.	Fair	Fair and frosty

Clouds

Every cloud is a weather sign.
Low clouds swiftly moving indicate coolness and rain.

Soft clouds, moderate winds, fine weather.
Hard-edged clouds, wind.
Rolled or ragged clouds, strong wind.
'Mackerel' sky, twelve hours dry.

Rain

Look out for rain when
The tree frog cries.
Fish swim near the surface.
Walls are unusually damp.
Flies are troublesome and sting sharply.
A slack rope tightens.
Smoke beats downward.
Sun is red in the morning.
There is a pale yellow sunset.

Rain with East wind is lengthy.
A sudden shower is soon over.
A slow rain lasts long.
Rain before seven, clear before eleven.
Sun drawing water, sure sign of rain.
A circle round the moon means 'storm.'

> When the grass is dry at night
> Look for rain before the light;
> When the grass is dry at morning light
> Look for rain before the night.

> When the dew is on the grass
> Rain will never come to pass.

Fog in the morning, bright sunny day.
Swallow flying high means clearing weather.
If the sun goes down cloudy Friday, sure of a clear Sunday.
Busy spiders mean fine weather.

The Winds

East wind brings rain.
West wind brings clear, bright, cool weather.
North wind brings cold.

South wind brings heat.

Birds fly high when the barometer is high, and low when the barometer is low.

Direction of Wind

The way to find which way the wind is blowing, if there is only very light breeze, is to throw up little bits of dry grass; or to hold up a handful of light dust and let it fall, or to suck your thumb and wet it all round and let the wind blow over it, and the cold side of it will then tell you which way the wind is blowing.

Weather Bureau

The Weather Bureau publishes a 'Classification of clouds,' in colours which may be had for the asking. If you are near one of the weather signal stations daily bulletins will be sent to camp upon request, also the weather map.

A set of flag signals run up each day will create interest. The flags are easily made, or may be purchased.

Keep a daily record of temperature. A boy in charge of the 'Weather Bureau' will find it to be full of interest, as well as to offer an opportunity to render the camp a real service. He will make a weather vane, post a daily bulletin board, keep a record of temperature, measure velocity of wind and rainfall.

If you have lost your bearings and it is a cloudy day, put the point of your knife blade on your thumb nail, and turn the blade around until the full shadow of the blade is on the nail. This will tell you where the sun is, and decide in which direction the camp is.

Points of Compass

Face the sun in the morning, spread out your arms straight from body. Before you is the east; behind you is the west; to your right hand is the south; to the left hand is the north.

A Home-made Weather Prophet

For a home-made barometer you need a clean, clear glass bottle. Take one drachm[1] each of camphor gum, saltpetre and ammonia salts, and dissolve them in thirteen drachms of pure alcohol. Shake till dissolved. Then pour in bottle and cork tightly. Hang the bottle of mixture against the wall facing north, and it will prove a perfect weather prophet. When the liquid is clear it promises fair weather. When it is muddy or cloudy it is a sign of rain. When little white flakes settle in the bottom it means that the weather is growing colder, and the thicker the deposit the colder it becomes. Fine, starry flakes foretell a storm, and large flakes are signs of snow. When the liquid seems full of little, threadlike forms that gradually rise to the top, it means wind and sudden storm.

Plant Barometers

The dandelion is an excellent barometer, one of the commonest and most reliable. It is when the blooms have seeded and are in the fluffy, feathery condition that its weather prophet facilities come to the fore. In fine weather the ball extends to the full, but when rain approaches, it shuts like an umbrella. If the weather is inclined to be showery it keeps shut all the time, only opening when the danger from the wet is past.

The ordinary clover and all its varieties, including the trefoil and the shamrock, are barometers. When rain is coming, the leaves shut together like the shells of an oyster and do not open again until fine weather is assured. For a day or two before rain comes their stems swell to an appreciable extent and stiffen so that the leaves are borne more upright than usual. This stem swelling when rain is expected is a feature of many towering grasses.

The fingers of which the leaves of the horse chestnut are made up keep flat and fanlike so long as fine weather is likely to continue. With the coming of rain, however, they droop, as if to offer less resistance to the weather. The scarlet pimpernel, nicknamed the 'poor man's weather glass', or wind cope, opens its flowers only to fine weather. As soon as rain is in the air it shuts up and remains closed until the shower or storm is over.

Bibliography

Talk About the Weather – Charles Barnard. Funk & Wagnalls Co. A little book of valuable hints and suggestions about the weather and the philosophy of temperature and rainfall in their relation to living things.

Woodcraft – Jones and Woodward. C. Arthur Pearson, Ltd. Contains an excellent chapter on weather lore in addition to a mass of valuable information on woodcraft.

20

Rainy Day Games and Suggestions

We knew it would rain for the poplars showed
The white of their leaves, and amber grain
Shrunk in the wind and the lightning now
Is tangled in tremulous skeins of rain.

(Aldrich)

Rainy days break the monotony of continuous sunshiny days. There is nothing that is so fascinating to a boy in camp as listening to the patter of the rain drops upon the roof of his canvas house, especially at night, if he is snug and warm in his blankets and the tent is waterproof. A rainy day is the kind of a day when the chess and checker enthusiasts get together. Games are rescued from the bottom of the trunk or box. Ponchos and rubber boots are now in popular favour. Thunder and lightning but add to the boys' enjoyment. What indescribable excitement there is in the shivers and shudders caused by an extra flash of lightning or a double fortissimo roll of thunder! There is also the delight, of playing in the puddles of water and wearing a bathing suit and enjoying a real shower bath.

To some boys it is repair day, rips are sewed up, buttons sewed on clothing, and for the initiated, the darning of socks. In camps with permanent buildings a big log fire roars in the fireplace, the boys sprawl on the floor with their faces toward the fire, and while the rain plays a tattoo[1] upon the roof some one reads aloud an interesting story, such as *Treasure Island*, *The Shadowless Man*, *The Bishop's Shadow*, or the chapters on 'The Beneficent Rain' and 'When the Dew Falls', from Jean M. Thompson's book, *Water Wonders*. It all depends upon one's viewpoint whether rainy days are delightful or disagreeable.

Surplus Energy

Boys are barometers. Restlessness is usually a sign of an approaching storm. The wise leader senses the situation and begins preparing his plans. If the rain is from the east and comes drizzling down, better plan a several day programme, for after the excitement of the first few hours' rain, the boys begin to loll around, lie on the cots, or hang around the kitchen and develop a disease known as

'Grouchitis.' During the first stages of the disease the boys are inactive and accumulate an over-supply of energy, which must find an outlet. Here is where the leader plays an important part in handling the case; he provides an outlet for the expenditure of this surplus energy by planning games demanding use of muscle and the expenditure of energy and noise. The big mess tent, or dining hall, is cleared and romping games are organised.

The games suggested are adapted for rainy days and selected from a catalogue of several hundred games.

Rainy Day Games

Few sports are better calculated than a potato joust to amuse boys on rainy days. It has all the joys of a combat, and yet, try as he will, there is no possibility for any boy to become rough.

Potato Joust

In the potato joust each warrior is armed with a fork, on the end of which is a potato. The combatants take their position in the centre of the playroom, facing each other. They should be separated by not less than three feet. Each must lift a leg from the floor (see illustration, opposite). The fighters may use their own discretion as to which leg shall be lifted from the floor and may hold it up with either hand they prefer. A small cushion placed under the knee will add materially to the comfort of the contestants.

The battle is decided by one of the warriors knocking the potato from his opponent's fork. Toppling over three times is also counted as defeat. If one of the knights is obliged to let go of his foot in order to keep his balance it is counted as a fall. Every time the battle is interrupted in this way, either of the contestants is at liberty to change the foot he is resting upon. If one of the warriors falls against the other and upsets him, it is counted against the one who is responsible for the tumble.

You are not likely to realise on your first introduction to a potato joust the amount of skill and practice required to really become expert in handling the fork. A slight turn of the wrist, a quick push and the practised knight will defeat the novice so deftly, so easily that you are amazed.

Move your fork as little as possible; long sweeping strokes are more likely to throw off your own potato than to interfere with that of your opponent.

The most dangerous stroke is one from underneath; always manoeuvre to keep your potato below that of your antagonist.

Handkerchief Tussle

Study the illustration opposite and see if you can discover a way for the boys to get apart. To make it really exciting, a number of couples should be set going

Above left: Handkerchief Tussle

Above right: Potato Joust

at once, and a 'second' on ice cream offered to the pair who get apart first. To separate, the boys have only to push the centre of one of the handkerchiefs under the loop made by the other handkerchief when it was tied about the wrist, and then carry the loop over the hand.

Rough-house is the expression used by the boy of today when he is describing a general scuffle, and he always smacks his lips over the word. But rough-house has its disadvantages, as many sprains and bruises can testify, and if the same amount of fun may be had from less trying amusement, an amusement, say, which is quite as energetic and quite as exciting, the boy of today will certainly adopt it in preference to rough-house.

Terrier Fight

A terrier fight is exciting, and it is funny – it is also energetic – and victory depends quite as much upon the skill of the fighter as upon his strength. Furthermore a terrier fight is not brutal. No boy will hurt himself while engaged in this sport. Two boys are placed facing each other in the centre of the room, hands clasped beneath the knees and a stick just under the elbows, as shown overleaf. Each contestant endeavours to push the other over; but as it requires considerable attention to keep the balance at all when in this position, the attack is no easy matter.

To give way suddenly is a manoeuvre almost sure to upset your adversary, but unfortunately it is very apt to upset you at the same time and only after considerable practice will you be able to overcome a man in this way. The pivot, a sudden swing to the right or left is safer, though not quite as effective. Always remember that the best terrier fighter invariably makes his opponent throw himself. Give way at some unexpected point, and unless he is a skilful man, he is sure to go over. Never try a hard push except in the last extremity when everything else has failed.

A terrier fight

A terrier fight consists of three one-minute rounds, with thirty seconds' rest between each round. The one scoring the largest number of falls during the time set is accounted the winner.

Circle Ball

A large circle of players throw a lawn tennis ball at one in the centre. The object of the player in the centre is to remain 'in' as long as possible without being hit. If he catches the ball in his hands it does not count as a hit. Whoever hits him with the ball takes his place. The player who remains 'in' longest wins.

Leg Wrestle

Lie down on the back, side by side, by twos, the feet of each boy of a two being beside the other boy's head. At the word 'Go!' each brings the leg nearest his opponent at right angles with his body and then lowers it. This may be done twice or three times, but the last time the leg is raised he should catch his opponent's and endeavour to roll him over, which is a defeat.

Hand Wrestling

Take hold of each other's right or left hand and spread the feet so as to get a good base. At the word 'Go!' each one endeavours to force his opponent to lose his balance, so as to move one of his feet. This constitutes a throw. The opponent's arm is forced quickly down or backward and then drawn out to the side directly away from him, thus making him lose his balance. The one moving his foot or touching his hand or any part of his body to the floor, so as to get a better base, is thrown. The throw must be made with the hand. It is thus not rulable to push with the head, shoulder or elbow.

Rooster Fight

The combatants are arranged facing each other in two front, open ranks. The first two 'opposites' at either or both ends, or if the floor is large enough all the opposites, may combat at the same time. The boys should fold their arms forward, and hop toward each other on one leg. The butting is done with the shoulder and upper arm, and never with the elbow, and the arm must remain folded throughout the combat. When the two adversaries meet, each attempts to push the other over, or make him touch to the floor the foot that is raised. When all have fought, the winners arrange themselves in two opposing ranks and renew the combat. This is done, until but one remains, and he is declared the victor.

Shoe and Jumper Race

The jumpers are placed at the opposite ends of the room. The boys start with their shoes on (laces out). A line is drawn in the middle of the room; here the contestants sit down and pull off their shoes), run to the jumpers and put them on. On the return trip they put their shoes on and finish with both shoes and jumpers on.

Peanut Relay Race

Boys are lined up in two columns, as in ordinary relay races. For each column two chairs are placed a convenient distance apart, facing one another, with a knife and a bowl half full of peanuts on one, and an empty bowl on the other. At the proper word of command the first boy on each side takes the knife, picks up a peanut with it, and carries the peanut on the knife to the farther bowl; upon his return the second boy does the same and so on. The second boy cannot leave until the first has deposited his peanut in the empty bowl, and has returned with the knife. Peanuts dropped must be picked up with the knife. Fingers must not be used either in putting the peanut on the knife or holding it there. The side, every member of which first makes the round, wins.

A Few Interesting Tests

You can't stand for five minutes without moving, if you are blindfolded.

You can't stand at the side of a room with both of your feet touching the wainscoting lengthwise.

You can't get out of a chair without bending your body forward or putting your feet under it, that is, if you are sitting squarely on the chair and not on the edge of it.

You can't crush an egg when placed lengthwise between your hands, that is, if the egg is sound and has the ordinary shell of a hen's egg.

You can't break a match if the match is laid across the nail of the middle finger of either hand and pressed upon by the first and third fingers of that hand, despite its seeming so easy at first sight.

Bibliography

Social Activities for Men and Boys – A.M. Chesley. Association Press. 295 ideas, games, socials and helpful suggestions.

Games for Everybody – May C. Hofman. Dodge Publishing Co. 200 pages of rare fun.

Education by Play and Games – G.E. Johnson. Ginn and Company, 90. A discussion of the meaning of play. Contains also a number of good games, graded according to ages or periods of child life.

Play – Emmett D. Angell. Little, Brown and Company. A very practical book, containing instruction for planning more than one hundred games, including eight games in the water.

21

Educational Activities

'Tis education forms the common mind;
Just as the twig is bent the tree's inclined.

(Pope)

A boy is better unborn than untaught.

(Gascoigne)

Camping should not be merely a time of loafing or 'having fun.' The boy who has returned from a camp, having learned some definite thing, whether it be different from the school curriculum or supplementary to his school work, has accomplished something and his outing has been of use to him. All play and no work makes Jack a dull boy, as well as 'all work and no play.' Recreative and constructive education forms a combination which appeals strongly to a boy. He would call it, 'doing things', and in the doing would have fun galore.

In addition to nature study, woodcraft, first-aid instruction and similar types of educational activities in vogue in boy's camps, there are many other forms of educational activities which boys can engage in during the camping season.

Whittlers' Club

A 'Whittlers' Club', organised to meet one hour several mornings a week, proved attractive to a group of boys in one camp. Under the leadership of a man who understood Sloyd[1] work the boys were taught how to handle a knife, and it is surprising how few boys really know how to handle this useful article found in every boy's pocket. They were also taught to know the different kinds of wood, bark, grain, and method of cutting and sawing wood for building and furniture purposes, etc. A popular model was a paper knife made of wild cherry. The bark was permitted to remain on the handle, while the other end was whittled evenly and smoothly for cutting leaves of books or magazines. With the aid of a pyrography set the name of the camp and that of the owner of the knife was burned on the handle.

Pyrography

Carved paddles, war clubs, hiking sticks, etc., were used to display the artistic ability of the boys who brought to camp pyrography sets. The camp name, date of hikes, miles travelled, and other interesting information was burned on these souvenirs. Shields containing the athletic records and names of honour boys were made and hung upon the walls of the permanent building.

Boat Building

In one large camp an experienced boatman was engaged, and under his direction three large dories were built by the boys. Plans were carefully worked out, lumber purchased, and details of boat construction explicitly explained. It took three weeks to build the boats, but no boats of the fleet were used and appreciated as much by the boys as these which represented so much of their own labour and time. Working plans and 'knocked down' material for building boats may be purchased from a number of firms. Building a boat during the winter by boys who are contemplating going camping, aids to the anticipation of the delightful summer time.

Plays

'The Player's Scene', from *Midsummer Night's Dream*, has been given several times outdoors with great success in the camps conducted by the writer. The boys were coached by a graduate of a School of Oratory, costumes were made by the boys out of all sorts of material, make-up was bought from a theatrical supply house and the scenery supplied by nature. Footlights were lanterns set in front of reflectors made from old tomato cans. The path leading to the natural amphitheatre was lighted by Japanese lanterns and the guests were seated on the ground. In the words of Hamlet, 'The Play's the Thing', and boys and visitors are always enthusiastic over the presentation, while the players get a new conception of Shakespeare's plays and writings. *Hiawatha* was given with equal enthusiasm and success.

Lantern Talks

Since the invention of the inexpensive Reflectoscope, illustrated talks in camp are now possible.. A number of the large camps have stereopticons. Lantern slides with accompanying lecture may be rented at reasonable rates. Any first-class firm dealing in lantern slides can furnish a number of valuable lectures with slides. A sheet hung between two trees on a dark night makes an excellent screen on which to show pictures.

Library

Every camp should have a library or at least a small collection of good books. In most cases arrangements can be made with a near-by library for the loan of books for a certain period of time. Camps having permanent buildings should 'grow' a library. The excellent library of 1,200 books in the camp of the writer was given by the boys.

Gummed book labels were sent to each boy with the suggestion that he paste them in books which he could bring to camp to present to the library. Some boys would bring as many as ten books from the home library, all good, readable books. The books are catalogued and a loan system established, under the 'Department of Education,' and the following rules govern the library and use of books:

1 Library open for one-half hour after dinner daily except on Sunday, when it will be open for one-half hour after breakfast.
2 Books can be kept out three days. If kept overtime a charge per day is made. Books may be renewed if returned on day due, otherwise the usual charge will be made.
3 From 9 o'clock a.m. to 12 o'clock a.m., and from 2 o'clock p.m., books may be taken away to read in the room, but must not be taken outside the building under any condition. Violation of this rule will deprive the violator of the use of the books for three days.
4 Please bring small change to pay fines.

Tutoring

The following announcement is sent by the writer to parents and boys concerning tutoring in camp:

Special Announcement of Tutoring.
Provides Opportunity For:
1 Those who, on account of illness or other unavoidable circumstances, have fallen behind their grade and wish to catch up by summer study.
2 Those who, on account of poor work or failure in examination, cannot be promoted unless they do special work during the vacation time.
3 Those who have not fully mastered a given subject and desire to review and strengthen themselves in the subject.
4 Those who wish to use their summer in order to earn an extra promotion.

Instruction:

Many of our camp leaders are college men and have the requisite scholarship to conduct the academic feature of the camp. The instruction is very largely individual and is given in the morning and does not interfere with the recreation life. The combination of study and recreation makes tutoring attractive and stimulating.

Subjects:

Any subject in the grammar or high school curriculum.

Time:

Two or three periods per week will be given to each subject.

An accurate record is kept of every boy being tutored, on a card and a duplicate sent to his parent at the close of the season.

Photography

To stimulate interest in photography, a contest is held during the latter part of the camping season for a cup, to be awarded to the boy securing the best collection of photographs of camp life. The award is determined upon: first, selection of subjects, and, second, execution of detail. Ribbon awards are given for the best individual photograph in these three classes: (a) portraits, (b) groups, (c) landscapes. The regulations governing the contest are:

1 Exposure, developing, and printing must be the work of the exhibitor.
2 Mounted or unmounted photographs may be submitted.
3 All photographs must be handed in before 12 o'clock noon (date inserted).

For camps having good dark rooms, the following rules may be suggestive:

1 Key to the dark room must be returned to the office immediately after using room and locking same.
2 If films are drying, inform the office of same, so that the next user may be notified and care taken not to disturb the films.
3 Room must be kept clean:
    (a) Do not wipe shelves with the hand towels.
    (b) Hang hand towels on nail provided.
    (c) Leave buckets and trays in clean condition.
    (d) Put paper, empty tubes, etc., in box provided for same and not upon the floor.

4 Use only the buckets provided, and not those used for kitchen or camp purposes.

5 Use only your own property and that provided by the camp, and never touch the property or films or plates of others.

Camp Paper

Every large camp has its official organ or camp paper. An editorial board is appointed, and the doings of the camp recorded in a permanent manner through the weekly issue or reading of the paper. Various names are given the paper, such as *The Camp Log, Dudley Doings, Seen and Heard, The Maskwa, The Wyanoka Log, Kinoe Kamper*. Some of these papers are printed and others are mimeographed and sold to the campers. Most of them, however, are written in a book and read at the camp fire.

Agriculture

Where a camp is located so as to be near a farm, opportunity should be given to city boys to study soil, rotation of crops, gardening, etc. In cooperation with the Department of Agriculture and under the leadership of a student of an Agricultural College, an experiment in raising vegetables may be tried in long-term camps. A plot of ground may be ploughed and harrowed, and sub-divided into as many plots as there are tents, each tent to be given a plot and each boy in the tent his 'own row to hoe,' the boy to make his own choice of seed, keep a diary of temperature, sunshine, rainfall, when the first blade appeared; make an elementary analysis of soil, use of fertiliser and other interesting data. Prepare for an exhibit of vegetables. Whatever the boys raise may be cooked and eaten at their table.

Forestry

The subject of forestry is akin to camping. Much valuable instruction may be given boys regarding the forests of the locality in which the camp is located, kind of land, character and use of woods, how utilised – conservatively or destructively – for saw timber, or other purposes, protection of forests, forest fires, etc.

Scoutcraft

The Handbook of the Boy Scouts is full of information regarding knot tying, signalling, tracking, use of compass, direction and time calculator, etc., which every boy should know. Scoutcraft would furnish recreational education for scores of boys.

Record Books

Boys like to carry home some permanent record of personal achievements while at camp, autographs of fellow campers, etc. A rather unique record is used by the boys at one camp. 'A Vacation Diary,' in the form of a vest pocket memorandum book, bound in linen, is published by Charles R. Scott, State Y.M.C.A. Committee, Newark, N. J.

Kites

Scientific kite flying is one of the best things a boy can indulge in. Hiye-Sho-To, a Japanese, gives this interesting information about kites.

To all Japanese the kite is symbolic of worthy, soaring ambitions, such as the work upward to success in school, or in trade, and so on. When a child is born, little kites are sent up by modest households to announce the arrival. Kites are also flown to celebrate birthdays. To lose a kite is considered an omen of ill-luck.

For the control of a box kite, I prefer the lightest steel wire to a cord. This wire is about the thickness of an ordinary pin, with a tensile strength at the point of breaking of quite three hundred pounds. In handling a kite with such a wire-ground connection, a boy should always have rough gloves on his hands, that the wire may not cut them.

Having a kite of this kind, or even two and three, so that on a single wire he can keep sending them higher and higher into the atmosphere, a boy can begin what we were wont to call in Yeddo our 'kite education.' First, he can make himself his own weather prophet. Self-registering thermometers are no longer very expensive. He can wire one of these to his kite, and, by knowing the length of wire he has in hand and the amount he pays out while the kite is up, ascertain just what the air temperature is 200 feet, 500 feet, 1,000 feet, 3,000 feet above him.

There are wind gauges of cheap construction, moisture gauges which will note the coming of rain, small cameras that will automatically take pictures while the kite is in the air, that may be attached to these kites, and from the work of which valuable information may be obtained.

The following instruction for making a box kite was given in *The American Boy*, April 1909:

 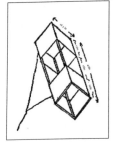

Far left: Kite 1

Left: Kite 2

Any boy can make a box kite. The material used may be any tough, light wood, such as spruce, cypress, bass-wood, or cedar. Cut four pieces 42 inches in length, and sixteen pieces 18 inches in length. The cuts show clearly how they are to be put together. Use glue and small brads at every point. The bridle cord is fastened 6 inches from each end of the box. This is best done before the cloth is put on the kite. Light cheese cloth may be used, and should be secured with glue and small brads at the last lap. When the cloth is in place paint it with thin varnish or glue to fill up the meshes and stretch it.

The reason why box kites made by boys have a tendency to lie down flat on the ground is that they are not proportioned correctly. The proportions given here are correct. The painting, decorating, and tinting are matters of personal taste and skill.

The principle of kite flying is simple. Air is a fluid like water, but on account of the many changes of temperature, to which it is subjected, it constantly changes its density and is found to consist of layers or strata. These layers are not all flat and parallel, but take every variety of shape as the clouds do. In flying a kite you simply pull it up one of those layers just as you would pull a sled or wagon up a hill. Always run facing the wind.

Aeroplanes

Aeroplane season is now a calendar event in the boy's life. Many boys are engaged in building these fascinating little ships of the air. *The Boy's Book of Model Aeroplanes*, by Francis A. Collins, Century Co. gives complete directions how to build these marvellous new toys. Form a club and conduct an 'Aviation' meet during the season.

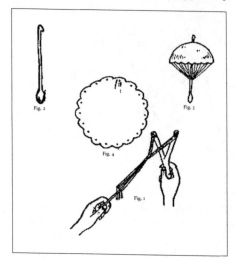

A parachute idea

Parachutes

The parachute, in its various forms, has always been a favourite with boys. The idea is to make an umbrella-shaped contraption out of tissue paper and a stick, so that when it descends from any considerable height it will open out and float slowly to the ground. This part is easy enough. The trouble has always been to get it up in the air high enough to repay one for his efforts in making it. The idea that a common sling shot had propelling power sufficient for this purpose led to experiments which proved that the idea was a happy one. The combination of sling shot and parachute makes a very fascinating outdoor amusement device. Every time you shoot it into the air you try to make it go higher than last time.

To make the parachute, get a tough stick about two feet long and whittle it to a shape similar to Fig. 2. The bottom must be heavy enough to fall first so that the parachute will fall in the right direction to be opened out. You can weight the end by tying a piece of lead or a spool on it. Cut your tissue paper to a shape shown in Fig. 2 and place a thread through every scallop. If the paper tears right through, a good plan is to reinforce the edges of the circle by pasting a strip of tough paper or muslin all around. A parachute made of silk or any fine mesh cloth will be much more lasting, but not quite so buoyant.

The sling shot is made with a rubber band, some string, and a forked stick. The greater its propelling power, the more successful will the toy be.

Box Furniture

Instead of using for firewood the boxes in which groceries, etc., are shipped to camp, have the boys make useful camp furniture from them. Get the book, *Box Furniture*, by Louise Brigham: The Century Co. It tells what to do with boxes, and how to make all sorts of convenient furniture.

Camp Clock

Mark the ground around the camp flag pole with white stones or stones whitewashed, like a sun dial. The sun's rays will cast the shadow of the pole so that the time of day may be accurately ascertained. (See illustration below) In the handbook of the Boy Scouts is the following description for making a Sun dial or Hunter's Clock:

> To make a sun dial prepare a smooth board about 15 inches across, with a circle divided into 24 equal parts, and a temporarily hinged pointer, whose upper edge is in the middle of the dial. Place on some dead level solid post or stump in the open. At night fix the dial so that the 12-o'clock line points exactly to North, as determined by the North or Pole Star. Then, using two temporary sighting sticks of exactly the same height (so as to permit sighting clear above the edge of the board), set the pointer exactly pointing to the Pole Star, that is, the same angle as the latitude of the place, and fix it there immovably. Then remove the two sighting sticks.

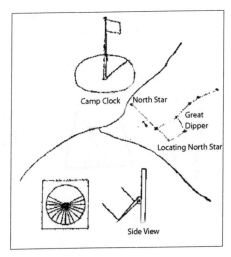

Sun dial or hunter's clock

Some Quotations to Burn or Paint on the Sun Dial:

> My face marks the sunny hours,
> What can you say of yours.

> Grow old along with me,
> The best is yet to be.

Translation of motto on Cathedral Sun dial, St. Augustine:

> The hours pass and we are held accountable.

The illustration shows how to locate the North or Pole Star.

Moccasins

F.O. Van Ness gives the following directions for making a pair of moccasins:

Fig. 1   Place foot on leather or canvas and draw outline of foot. Turn same and make pattern for other foot.

Fig. 2   Distance GB equals length of foot plus one inch; distance AC equals width across instep plus one-half inch; cut DF halfway between B and G; cut EG halfway between A and C. Cut piece reverse of this for other moccasin. Place B of Fig. 2 to B of Fig. 1, and sew overhand with wax cord the edges from B to A and B to C, bringing A and C of Fig. 2 together at A of Fig. 1. Sew AG to CG.

Fig. 3   is the tongue and DF of Fig. 3 is sewed to DF of Fig. 2. Cut pairs of half-inch slits a, b, c, d in Fig. 2, and run lace through.

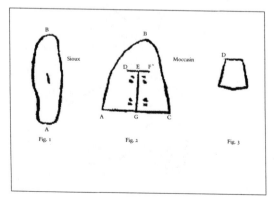

Sioux Moccasin

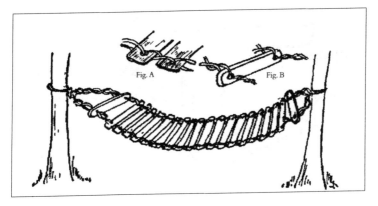

Rough and ready hammock

Hammock-Making

For the afternoon 'siesta' make a 'rough-and-ready' hammock, by taking apart a flour barrel or sugar barrel, and in the end of each stave bore a three-quarter inch hole with a heated poker, or bit and auger. Then lace thin rope (clothes line is good) through the holes. This can be accomplished easily by noting method of lacing in figure 'A.' The stay-blocks 'B' should be 12 inches long. Figure 'C' shows hammock ready for use.

A Toboggan

Get a cheese box. Knock in the end very carefully, so as not to split it, pull out all the nails and lay it flat, and you have a piece of very thin board about 4-1/2 feet long and 11 inches wide. Next take a piece of inch plank of same width as the cheese box, and three feet in length, and to this fasten the unrolled cheese box by using small lath nails, letting one end curl up over the plank. To the edge of this protruding piece of cheese box tack a narrow strip of wood. Tie a heavy cord to its ends, run the cord through the two hooks screwed into the planks and draw down the end until it is curved just right. The illustration shows how it is made.

Handy Funnel

A funnel may be made by taking an ordinary envelope and cutting off the part shown in dotted lines as in the illustration. Then clip a little off the point, open out, and you have an excellent funnel.

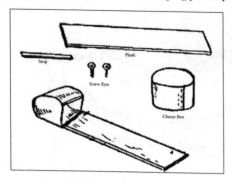

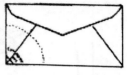

Left: Home made toboggan

Above: A handy funnel

Onion Ink

Dip a pen in an onion and press until the juice comes; then, with plenty of juice on the pen, write your message. To read it warm it over the fire, when the writing will stand out clearly.

Bibliography

List of books on handcraft and construction:

Field and Forest Handy Book – D.C. Beard. Charles Scribner's Sons.
Jack of All Trades – D.C. Beard. Charles Scribner's Sons.
The Boy Pioneers – D.C. Beard. Charles Scribner's Sons.
The Boy Craftsman – A. Neely Hall. Lothrop, Lee & Shepard Co.
Woodworking for Beginners – C.G. Wheeler. Putnam and Company.
Amateur Mechanics, Nos. 1 and 2. Popular Mechanics.
How to Build a Biplane Glider – A.P. Morgan. Spon & Chamberlain.
Problems in Furniture Making – Fred D. Crawshaw. Manual Arts Press.
Box Furniture – Louise Brigham. Century Co.
The Boys' Book of Model Aeroplanes – Francis A. Collins. Century Co.

22

Honour Emblems and Awards

Honour is purchased by the deeds we do;
* * * honour is not won,
Until some honourable deed be done.

(Marlowe)

Non-Competitive Awards

Achievement and cooperation based upon altruism, should be the underlying principles in determining the giving of emblems and awards. To give every boy an opportunity to do his best to measure up to the camp standard, is the thing desired in the awarding of emblems. Non-competitive tests are being recognised as the best lever of uplift and the most effective spur in arousing the latent ability of boys. The desire to down the other fellow is the reason for much of the prevailing demoralisation of athletics and competitive games. Prizes should not be confused with 'honours.' An honour emblem should be representative of the best gift the camp can bestow and the recipient should be made to feel its worth. The emblem cannot be bought, it must be won.

Dudley Plan

Camp Dudley has the distinction of introducing the honour system in boys' camps. Boys pass tests which include rowing, swimming, athletics, mountain climbing, nature study, carpenter work, manual labour, participation in entertainments, 'unknown' point (unknown to the camp, given secretly to the boy) and securing the approval of the leaders, in order to win the 'C D.' After winning this emblem, the boys try to win the camp pennant, the tests for which are graded higher.

Camp Eagle

'The Order of the Adirondack Camp Eagle' is established at Camp Adirondack for boys who qualify in the following tests:

Obedience is required to the few camp rules; promptness is required at the regular bugle calls – reveille, assembly for exercise, mess call, and tattoo and taps – and erect posture is required at meals. In addition to this there is a 'general personal' standard (embracing neatness at meals and courtesy, etc.). Boys coming up to the standard are initiated into the order and receive the emblem – the bronze eagle button. Boys who reach an especially high standard receive the silver eagle. Boys reaching this higher degree may compete for the golden eagle, the highest camp honor. To obtain this it is necessary for a boy to swim a hundred yards, do the high dive (about 12 feet), be able to row well and paddle a canoe skillfully, recognise and name twenty-five trees, and pass a practical examination in other nature work and in practical camping and woodcraft, and answer questions in physical training and care of the body along lines covered in camp-fire talks.

'The Order of the Phantom Square' was organised at one camp for boys who succeed in qualifying in the tests named below:

Bronze, Silver and Gold Pins are awarded as follows:
Bronze – 60 points, 15 in each division.
Silver – 80 points, 20 in each division.
Gold – 100 points, 25 in each division.

Physical. 30 points possible:

Event	A (16–17)	B (14–15)	C (12–13)	Points
*1. Run 100 yd	12 sec	13 sec	7.2 sec (50yd)	1
* 2. Run 440 yd	1:13	1:25	1:34	1
*3. Running broad jump	14ft	13ft	11ft	1
*4. Running high jump	4ft	3ft 10in	3ft 6in	1
*5. Shot put 8lb	30ft	25ft	20ft	1
*6. Swim 25 yd	19 sec	22 sec	25 sec	1
*7. Swim on back 25 yd	—	—	—	1
*8. Swim 100 yd	—	—	—	1
*9. Dive in acceptable form	—	—	—	1

	4:20	4:25	5:10	1
*10. Row one mile	4:20	4:25	5:10	1
*11. Life saving test 70–79; 80–89; 90–100	—	—	—	3–5
+12. Calisthenic drill 8, 11, 14 times	—	—	—	1–3
+13. Early plunge in lake 8, 11, 14 times	—	—	—	1–3
*14. Walk 10 miles	—	—	—	2
+15. Cleanliness	—	—	—	1–5

Social Activity	Points
*16. Teach other boys in aquatics, athletics, or mental test	1–5
*17. Perform other good turns to individuals	1–5
+18. Congeniality with camp mates	1–4
+19. Neatness in care of personal property, tent and table	1–5
+20. Promptness in responding to bugle calls, signals and camp duties	1–3
*21. Participating acceptably in evening entertainments	1–5
*22. Participating acceptable in camp orchestra or glee club	3

Mental test	Points
*23. Pass written test in life-saving examination with grade of 70–79, 80–89, or 90–100	3–5
*24. Name and describe different kinds of trees and birds	1–5
*25. Name and point out star groups	1–3
*26. Answer questions on camp-fire talks	1–4
*27. Read and orally answer questions on 'Youth to Manhood'	1–5
*28. Read and tell story of other acceptable books	1–3
*29. Compose an acceptable song or yell for camp	5

Moral activity	Points
*30. Daily Bible reading with written answers to questions	1—5
+31. Reverence at religious exercises	1—3
+32. Attendance at Church on Sundays during camp	3
+33. Cheerful and faithful performance of camp duties	1—5
+34. Extra volunteer service at camp	1—5
+35. Self-control	1—4
+36. General conduct and disposition	1—5

Tests marked thus (*) are judged by certain leaders delegated for the purpose. Tests marked thus (+) are judged by all tent leaders for boys in their tents.

After a candidate has won the requisite number of points for the first degree, a unanimous vote of all leaders in council assembled, is necessary, after which, a solemn ceremony of initiation is conducted.

The Honour Emblem is given to all who win a total of at least thirty points covering all the tests.

Flag of Honour

One camp's spirit is developed through the 'Flag of Honour,' which is awarded each day to the tent scoring the highest number of points, as follows: Every boy up and in line at 3 minutes after 7, scores 5 points for his tent; the morning dip, 5 points; tent inspection, 100 points for perfect; winning in athletic and aquatic meet, 25 points; second, 20; third, 15; fourth, 10; and fifth, 5. On a winning cricket team, 5 points and amateur stunt, 10 points.

Green Rag Society

Another camp has the following elaborate plan: The camp emblem itself represents the first degree and the camper must be in camp for one full week before he can wear it. The emblem is a brown triangle with a large E placed upon it with a green background. A green bar is added for each year spent in camp. The second, third and fourth degrees are indicated by a small green star, to be placed at the points of the triangle, beginning at the lowest point, then the upper left, then the upper right. The second degree will be awarded by the first star, the third degree by the second star, also entitling the winner to membership in the 'Brown Rag' Society. The fourth degree will be awarded by the third star and the winner be entitled to membership in the 'Green Rag' Society.

Membership in the 'Green Rag' Society is the highest honour the camp can bestow. The following are the requirements for the higher degrees.

Requirements For The Second Degree

1 To catch a one-pound fish from the largest lake on camp.
2 To catch a one-pound fish from any other lake while at camp.
3 To row a boat (passing the rowing test).
4 To be able to swim 50 yards.
5 To be able to walk one mile in 11 minutes.
6 To be able to run 100 yards in 14 seconds.
7 To be able to start three consecutive fires with three consecutive matches in the woods, with fuel found in the woods; one of the fires to be built in a damp place. If one fire fails, the entire test must be repeated.
8 To bring in mounted five different butterflies.
9 To bring in mounted five different moths.
10 To bring in mounted five different beetles.
11 To collect and press 25 different wild flowers.
12 To jump 6 feet in standing broad jump.

Requirements For The Third Degree

1 To be able to start a fire with a fire drill, the fuel and material used to be found in the woods.
2 To be able to tell the correct time by the sun at least twice a day.
3 To be able to swim 200 yards.
4 To be able to row a boat one mile in ten minutes.
5 To measure the correct height of a tree without climbing it.
6 To be able to tie and untie eight different standard knots.
7 To catch a two-pound fish.
8 To be able to know and name fifteen different trees in the woods.
9 To be able to perform on a stunt night acceptably.
10 To be able to know and name 25 different birds as seen around the camp.
11 To lead in the Evening Devotions at least twice.
12 To run 100 yards in 13 seconds.

Requirements For The Fourth Degree

1 To catch a three-pound fish.
2 To be able to run 100 yards in 11 seconds.
3 To be able to run 100 yards in 12 seconds.
4 To conduct Evening Devotions.
5 To teach one boy how to swim (test one hundred feet).

6 To influence one boy into the Christian life.
7 To know and to name 25 different trees as found in the woods.
8 To be able to make twelve standard knots in a rope.
9 To conquer one bad habits while at camp.
10 To accomplish at least one definite piece of service as prescribed by the camp.
11 To become a member of the camp council.
12 To be able to jump 16 feet in the running broad Jump.

The tests in Camps Durrell and Becket are based upon Baden-Powell's book, *Scouting for Boys*, and have proven very successful. They are as follows:

Honour Plan

Discipline
1 Doing camp duty promptly, efficiently and cheerfully. (5 points.)
2 Participating promptly in preparing tents, baggage and beds for inspection. (4 points.)
3 Loyalty to captain in all games. (5 points.)

Observation
1 Observe the ways of birds, animals and people and jot down a sketch of them in a notebook. (3 points.)
2 Take a walk and upon return to the camp write upon the following six subjects.
   (a) Nature of by-ways of paths.
   (b) Different kinds of trees you noticed.
   (c) People you met.
   (d) Peculiar smells of plants.
   (e) Kind of fences you saw.
   (f) Sounds you heard. (3 points.)

3 Observe sanitary and hygienic disorder and correct the same. (5 points.)
4 After the reading aloud of a story write an account of it. (3 points.)

Woodcraft
1 Observe the tracks of birds and animals and distinguish them. (2 points.)
2 Identify fifteen birds, or fifteen trees, or fifteen flowers, or fifteen minerals. (2 points.)
3 Tie a square knot, a weaver's knot, a slip knot, a flemish coop, a bowline, a half, timber clove, boom hitches, stevedore and wall end knots, blackwall and catspaw turn and hitch hook hitches. (2 points.)

4 Make a 'star' fire and cook a meal upon it for the boys of your tent. (3 points.)

5 Find the south at any time of day by the sun with the aid of a watch. (1 point.)

6 Estimate the distance across water. (1 point.)

7 Judge the time of day by the sun. (1 point.)

8 Read the signs of the weather by the sun, wind and clouds. (2 points.)

9 Make something useful for the camp. (5 points.)

Health

1 Promptness, erect carriage and earnestness in setting up drill. (3 points.)

2 Gain made in physical development during the time in camp. (2 points.)

3 Essay upon the camp-fire talks on 'Personal Hygiene.' (3 points.)

4 Care of tent, clothing and baggage, in dry and wet weather. (3 points.)

5 Cleanliness of person. (3 points.)

6 Proper eating at meals. (5 points.)

7 Win first place in the athletic or aquatic events. (2 points.)

Chivalry

(Among the laws of the Knights was this: 'Chivalry requireth that youth should be trained to perform the most laborious and humble offices with cheerfulness and grace: and to do good unto others.')

1 Do a good turn to somebody every day. (3 points.)

2 Control tongue and temper. (5 points.)

3 Participate in some entertainment. (2 points.)

4 Secure the approval of the leaders. (2 points.)

5 Promptness in attending Chapel services. (2 points.)

Saving Life

1 Be able to swim fifty yards and return without stopping. (1 point.)

2 Pass the examinations in Life Saving and First Aid Work by written and demonstration work. (5 points.)

3 Row from wharf to a given point and back in a given time. (1 point.)

Patriotism

1 Respect for the British flag at raising and colours. (5 points.)

2 Memorise the national anthem. (1 point.)

3 Write an essay explaining the plan of governing your own town and city. (2 points.)

4 Write in your own words what you think citizenship means. (2 points.)

5 Describe upon paper some historic spot or building near your home and its connection with the making of Britain. (1 point.)

NOTE. – Each boy must win 90 points out of a possible 100 to secure the honour emblem. Leaders will be appointed to take charge of the different tests, to whom the boys will report when they qualify in the tests and receive their points. The final decision in the giving of the honour emblem is made at a full meeting of the Camp Council.

The honour emblem consists of a white 'swastika'[1] cross with garnet felt D for Durrell and B for Becket. Boys who fail to secure the emblem in one season are credited with points which hold good the next season. The Honour Pennant is awarded only to those who render special service to the camp.

The camp emblem is a garnet solid triangle with the initial of the camp in white felt upon it. A white bar placed above the triangle represents the attendance, one bar is given for each year. The Senior leader's emblem is a white felt disc with a garnet felt triangle, and the Junior leader's emblem, a garnet felt disc with a white felt triangle.

Campers will find enough suggestions in these outlines to develop systems of their own which will help in the all-round development of the boy.

Camp Kineo Cup

Some camps prefer the awarding of what may be called 'proficiency cups.' At Camp Kineo a silver cup is awarded to the boy in each division who is the best all-round fellow, considering manly qualities, loyalty to camp, deportment, behaviour under all conditions, skill in athletics, aquatics, tennis, cricket, and all other sports, self-control, temperament, popularity with boys and good standing with counsellors. The judges are the Director and Camp Council, whose decision counts for 60 per cent toward the final award, the boys not competing deciding the other 40 per cent toward the final award.

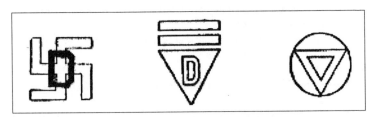

Honour, Camp, Leader

Hall of Fame

At Camp Wildmere there is a 'Hall of Fame.' Votes are taken for the most respected leader and the most respected boy, the most popular leader and boy; the boy who has done the most for the camp and the boys; the most courteous boy, neatest boy, best-built boy, brightest boy, favourite in games; neatest in tent; best all-round camper; boy who talks least about himself; the one with the best table manners; the quietest boy, most generous boy, handsomest boy, best-natured boy and the camp humourist.

Packing Up

Farewell, wild hearth where many logs have burned;
  Among your stones the fireweed may grow.
The brant[1] are flown, the maple-leaves have turned,
  The goldenrod is brown – and we must go.

(Arthur Guiterman)

The Last Night

The last night in a boys' camp should be the best of all the nights. It is usually a night of reminiscence. Around the camp fire or log fire in the 'Lodge,' all the campers gather and rehearse the good times of the days that have passed all too quickly – those days of close intimacy of tent life, where boys of different tastes, temperaments and dispositions were thrown together, where life's great lessons of give and take were learned and where character was put to the test! Friendships have been formed which will last through life. The same group of fellows will never come together again. The director, perhaps as no other person, realises the importance of making this night one of permanent impression, and his 'good-by' talk to the fellows will reiterate the 'why' of camping and emphasise the taking home of the spirit of good which has prevailed and the making it count for the best things in home, school, factory and church life of those boys who enjoyed the benefits of the camp.

All the favourite songs of the camp are sung, the leaders make 'speeches,' and the boys have an opportunity of telling what camp life has done for them. As the fire dies down the bugler off in the distance plays 'God Be With You Till We Meet Again'; silence – and then 'taps.'

Packing Up

There is just as much need of system and care in breaking camp and packing up, as in opening camp. Chas. R. Scott at Camp Wawayanda issues to each leader the following letter of instructions, which may be of help to those in charge of large camps.

Letter Of Instruction To Leaders

DEAR FRIEND – Will you kindly help me break camp by carrying out the following instructions:

1 Have all your boys return all books to the librarian not later than Thursday morning, and tools to the shop by the same time.

2 Encourage your helpers to loosen the side walls of tent early Friday morning, if clear, and fasten guy ropes so that canvas will dry if damp.

3 Take out all the pegs which fasten the side walls, clean off dirt and place in boxes at boat house.

4 Take down the board in your tent, take out all nails; straighten them and place in proper boxes in shop. Then take board to the boat house. Leave the rope over the ridge pole untied.

5 Take out all nails and screws in the upright poles of your tent and bunks, and place in boxes in shop.

6 Empty the oil and clean lantern and return to the boat house. Take bunks to the lodge and let us know the condition of each.

7 See that all paper and old things in and around the tent are picked up and placed on the fire for that purpose.

8 After Bible study we will take down all tents. We should like you to delegate one fellow to each upright pole, one to each of the four corner guy ropes, and then follow instructions as the bugle blows.

9 Take all rope on the trees to headquarters.

10 Kindly answer the following questions regarding your tent:
   a. Are all the poles properly marked with tent number?
   b. Does tent leak? If so, where?
   c. Is the ridge pole in good condition?
   d. Does front and rear of tent close securely?
   e. Does it need new fasteners for tying up?

   Anything else you have noticed during the time you have been in the tent; please make a memorandum of same on back of this sheet.

11 Return camp keys, if you have them, to headquarters before leaving.

We would be pleased to have you write on the back of this sheet any suggestions you have for the improvement of camp for next season. Thanking you personally for your help and trusting to have your cooperation and that of your boys until the close of camp, I remain, Sincerely yours,

Last Words

The day before camp breaks, each boy should pack his trunk or box neatly, leaving at the top the things needed to make the homeward journey, with room for his blankets. If the packing is left until the last day, confusion will result and temper be sorely tried.

Permanent buildings should be securely safeguarded against the severity of the winter and the breaking in of thieves. All kitchen utensils should be thoroughly cleaned and dried. If they are put away moist rust will eat holes. Give the stove a good coat of old grease and cover with burlap or old canvas. Hang the tents in bags where the squirrels and rats cannot get at them. When camp is closed it should be in such condition that it would require but a few hours to reopen and make ready for the next outing.

Endnotes

Chapter 3
1   Dr Chas. E.A. Winslow – Camp Conference, p. 58.
2   Thou shalt have a place also without the camp, whither thou shalt go forth abroad:
    And thou shalt have a paddle upon thy weapon; and it shall be, when thou wilt
    ease thyself abroad, thou shalt dig therewith, and shalt turn back and cover that
    which cometh from thee: For the LORD thy God walketh in the midst of thy
    camp, to deliver thee, and to give up thine enemies before thee; therefore shall thy
    camp be holy: that he see no unclean thing in thee, and turn away from thee.

Chapter 4
1   Cloth case for a mattress or pillow or a light mattress without springs.
2   Narrow strip of wood for flooring.
3   Smooth, heavy pasteboard.

Chapter 5
1   Personal baggage.

Chapter 6
1   E.M. Robinson, *Association Boys*, June 1902.

Chapter 7
1   Flat rings of iron or rope are pitched at a stake with points for encircling it. A ring
    used in this game.
2   Sentinel's challenge. On the alert; vigilant.
3   Signal on a drum or bugle to summon soldiers to their quarters at night.
    Continuous, even drumming or rapping.

Chapter 8
1   Walter M. Wood in Association Boys, June 1907.
2   Monotonous talk filled with platitudes. Hypocritically pious language.

Chapter 9
1   About 1/4 of a barrel or 9 gallons (34 litres).

Chapter 10

1 Dr. G. Stanley Hall, 'Camp Conference Report', p. 40

Chapter 13

1 This chapter was written in 1911. Many observations and suggestions are obsolete, if not dangerous or illegal.
2 Catarrh: Inflammation of mucous membranes in nose and throat.
3 Ataxia: Loss of coordinated muscular movement.
4 Collodion: Flammable, colourless or yellowish syrupy solution of pyroxylin, ether, and alcohol, used as an adhesive to close small wounds and hold surgical dressings, in topical medications, and for making photographic plates.

Chapter 14

1 Cloth coated with adhesive substance to cover cuts or scratches on the skin.

Chapter 15

1 Thole-pin: Pairs of wooden pegs set in the gunwales as an oarlock.
2 Painter: Rope attached to the bow for tying up when docking or towing.

Chapter 17

1 Emmett D. Angell in Play, p. 19.
2 A nock is the groove at either end of a bow for holding the bowstring or the notch in the end of an arrow that fits on the bowstring.

Chapter 19

1 Dram, drachma; drachm; U.S. Customary System equal to 1/16 of an ounce or 27.34 grains (1.77 grams). Apothecary weight equal to 1/8 of an ounce or 60 grains (3.89 grams).

Chapter 20

1 Signal on a drum or bugle to summon soldiers to their quarters at night. Continuous, even drumming or rapping.

Chapter 21

1 Manual training developed in Sweden, using woodworking tools.

Chapter 22

1 The swastika is an ancient religious symbol, a Greek cross with the ends of the arms bent at right angles. It was adopted by the Nazi party under Adolf Hitler in 1935. This book was written 22 years earlier.

Chapter 23

1 Brant: Dark wild goose of the Arctic having a black neck and head.

General Bibliography

Boy-Life and Self Government – Fiske. Association Press.
Boy-Training – Symposium. Association Press.
Youth – Hall. Appleton and Company.
Winning the Boy – Merrill. Revell and Company.
The Boy Problem – Forbush. Pilgrim Press.
Up Though Childhood – Hubbell. Putnam and Company.
Growth and Education – Tyler. Houghton, Mifflin Company.

Suggested articles on 'camping' in *Association boys*:

'A Course in Camping' – Edgar M. Robinson. Feb. 1902.
'The Sanitary Care of a Boys' Camp' – Elias G. Brown, M.D. April and June 1902.
'Seventeen Seasons in One Boys' Camp' – G.G. Peck. April 1902.
'Association Boys' Camps' – Edgar M. Robinson. June 1902.
'Following Up Camp' – Editorial. October 1902.
'What Men Think of Camp' – Edgar M. Robinson. June 1903.
'Fun Making at Camp' – C.B. Harton. June 1903.
'Educational Possibilities at Camp' – F.P. Speare. June 1903.
'Bible Study at Camp' – Raymond P. Kaighn. June 1903.
'Simple Remedies at Camp' – Elias G. Brown, M.D. June 1903.
'Tuxis System' – H.L. Smith. April 1904.
'Life at Camp Dudley' – Raymond P. Kaighn. June 1905.
'Life-Saving Crew' – F.H.T. Ritchie. June 1905.
'Summer Camps' – Frank Streightoff. June 1905.
'Wawayanda Camp' – Chas. R. Scott. June 1907.
'Objectives in Camps for Boys' – Walter M. Wood. June 1907.

Index